Realm
of the
Immortals

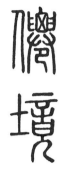

Realm

of the

Immortals

Daoism

in the Arts

of China

Stephen Little

The Cleveland

Museum of Art

February 10–

April 10, 1988

Published by

The Cleveland Museum of Art

in cooperation with

Indiana University Press

Cover: [21] JADE MINIATURE MOUNTAIN.
Nephrite, H. 17.5 cm. Qing dynasty,
eighteenth century. Anonymous Memorial
Gift CMA 41.594

Copyright 1988 by
The Cleveland Museum of Art
11150 East Boulevard
Cleveland, Ohio 44106

Distributed by
Indiana University Press
10th and Morton Streets
Bloomington, Indiana 47405

Editor: Jo Zuppan
Photographer: Nicholas Hlobeczy
Assistant: Stephen Kovacik
Design: Laurence Channing
Assistant: Richard Sarian

Library of Congress Cataloging-in-Publication Data

Little, Stephen, 1954-
  Realm of the immortals: Daoism in the arts of China / Stephen Little.
    p.   cm.
  Catalogue of an exhibition held Feb. 10-Apr. 10, 1988, at the Cleveland Museum of Art
  Bibliography: p.
  Includes index.
  ISBN 0-910386-92-7
  1. Art objects, Taoist—China—Exhibitions. 2. Art objects,
Chinese—Exhibitions. 3. Painting, Taoist—China—Exhibitions.
4. Painting, Chinese—Exhibitions. 5. Cleveland Museum of Art
—Exhibitions. I. Title
NK1678.T36L58 1987   87-35473
704.9'4899514'09—dc19   CIP

Contents

Foreword

The beliefs and superstitions of the earliest Chinese peoples were deeply influenced by the importance of the land and the forces of nature—hardly a surprise in an agricultural society—and by a great reverence for and concern about the well-being of the spirits of the deceased. Indeed, for the most part the earliest arts of the Chinese were created to nurture and propitiate the spirits of the deceased, for their well-being was a primary concern.

Written statements of faith and morality were slow to emerge, but finally within a short period two philosophies were articulated. In the early fifth century BC, the philosopher Confucius sought to define a system that was essentially a synthesis of the earlier traditional beliefs, based upon an optimistic humanism. Confucianism readily found an audience and became focal in the development of Chinese society and politics. Although its origins are not as clear, a second philosophy, called Daoism, emerged at approximately the same time. Also influenced by previous beliefs, this highly mystic system sought to articulate a point-of-view supporting its adherents in their search to establish man's place in the greater order of things. It advocated the achievement of harmony with those forces through intense spiritual exercises. In the next few centuries each of these indigenous philosophies went through countless developments; man's eternal need to organize the practices of faith inevitably made the mystic more mundane. However, they remained the dominant religious forces in China until, about 700 years later, the third major religious faith of the Chinese people, Buddhism, arrived from India. Thus, finally the three systems of belief that were to dominate China for centuries were in place.

Americans have long marveled at the grandeur of Chinese burial art, and many fine examples are found in this country's public collections. Understandably, therefore, Cleveland enthusiastically welcomed the opportunity to present the spectacular group of terra-cotta tomb sculptures in the exhibition *Quest for Eternity* lent by the People's Republic of China. To suggest the breadth of Chinese funerary art, the Museum also organized a modest exhibition, *Treasures for the Yellow Springs*, drawn from its own holdings, to complement the major loan exhibition. Since neither show deals directly with the complexities of an ancient doctrine little-known in the West, Stephen Little proposed *Realm of the Immortals: Daoism in the Arts of China* as an appropriate exhibition to enhance our appreciation of the Chinese loans. Using a relatively small group of objects—largely part of the Museum collection, a number of them never before published—he successfully conveys in considerable depth the tales and the point-of-view of the Daoist philosophy. This exhibition and its catalogue, we trust, complement the great objects lent by the Chinese People's Republic, even as they encourage a more perceptive understanding of the spiritual beliefs of one of the most remarkable cultures of all times.

Evan H. Turner

Acknowledgements

To mount a modest exhibition on the theme of Daoism in the arts of China is vii akin to describing in several pages the history of any complex and long-lived philosophy: one risks both lacunae in subject matter and errors of interpretation. This being understood, the responsibility for such faults is solely mine.

Notwithstanding, I would like to thank the following individuals for their generous assistance in this project: Marjorie Williams for providing the initial idea for the exhibition; Eliza Hatch for her research on the Eight Immortals and many hours of combing photographic archives for Daoist images in Chinese art; Nadine Tymon for writing the text of the entry on the bronze mirror depicting Xiwangmu; Hun Lee for deciphering the inscription on the Cheng Junfang ink cake; Laurence Channing, Emily S. Rosen, Cathy D'Addario, and Richard Sarian for the production of this volume; Jo Zuppan for her helpful criticism and editing; Nicholas Holbeczy for his photography; Jean Cassill for logistical support; Nancy Grossman for typing; the members of the library staff for their continual and well-organized assistance in all matters relating to research; and Joseph Finizia, designer, and the utility crew for the installation. I would particularly like to thank Mrs. A. Dean Perry, Mr. and Mrs. Wan-go H. C. Weng, and Ssu Isabel and I-hsüeh Hugo Weng for their generosity in loaning key paintings and calligraphy to the exhibition.

S.L.

Daoism: An Historical Introduction

Figure I. *Laozi Encountering Yin Xi at the Han'gu Pass.* Hanging scroll, ink and light colors on paper. Shang Xi, early fifteenth century, Ming dynasty. MOA Museum, Atami, Japan.

Dao in Chinese means a road or a way, and is often translated into English as "the Way." The Dao is the Way of all things; it represents both the machinations and ultimate source of everything in the universe. The Dao is often described as the void from which all reality emerges; in the Dao, all opposites are unified. The individual attuned to this truth concentrates on living in harmony with nature and the Dao that underlies it.

According to tradition, the first sage of Daoism was Laozi, who lived during the late Zhou dynasty (eleventh-third centuries BC; Figure I and [1]).[1] The book attributed to Laozi, *The Way and Its Power (Daode Jing)*, became the fundamental text of Daoism and is now believed to have been written during the fourth century BC. Originally it was as much a guide for the behavior of a ruler as a metaphysical text demonstrating the relativity of human experience.[2]

Defining the Dao is necessarily difficult. While pervading reality, the Dao is intangible and mysterious, and in describing it in words (by nature limited), one is rarely talking about it, according to Laozi. The first line of the *Daode Jing* thus reads: "The Dao that can be spoken of is not the true Dao." The paradox expressed in this and the following passage is characteristic of the language of the *Daode Jing:*

If one looks for Dao, there is nothing solid to see
If one listens for it, there is nothing loud enough to hear
Yet if one uses it, it is inexhaustible.[3]

The Dao therefore has a power that those with sufficient moral virtue can use to transform reality. The practical side of the *Daode Jing* is illustrated in this passage, in which the author describes the sagacious court officials of antiquity:

Of old those that were the best officers of Court
Had inner natures subtle, abstruse, mysterious, penetrating,
Too deep to be understood.
And because such men could not be understood
I can but tell of them as they appeared to the world:
    Circumspect they seemed, like one who in winter crosses a stream,
Watchful, as one who must meet danger on every side.
Ceremonious, as one who pays a visit
Yet yielding, as ice when it begins to melt.
Blank, as a piece of uncarved wood
Yet receptive as a hollow in the hills.[4]

After the *Daode Jing*, the second great Daoist book of antiquity was the *Zhuangzi*, believed to have been written in the early third century BC.[5] The title is also the name of the philosopher to whom the book is attributed. Zhuangzi introduced a new sardonic spirit into Daoist thought. He criticized Confucius

Figure II. *Fanghu, Isle of the Immortals.* Hanging scroll, ink and colors on silk. Wang Yun, 1652-1735 or later, Qing dynasty. Nelson-Atkins Museum, Kansas City.

2

(late sixth-early seventh century BC), for example, and branded as narrow that great social philosopher's preoccupation with correct human behavior. Zhuangzi saw human affairs as a dream and, through examples, demonstrated that human assumptions about reality are often arbitrarily deduced. His paragons were taken from antiquity and his own time, and their words and actions often had a political overtone.

The chapter entitled "Giving Away a Throne" contains several tales in which emperors of antiquity sense that their virtue is insufficient to rule. They resolve to seek out pure and unsullied farmers and fishermen, and offer them their thrones. When they do, however, these recluses usually laugh at the emperor and refuse his offer, thus illustrating the Daoist contempt for high office and politics.

The *Zhuangzi* is one of the earliest texts to discuss the Daoist ideal of the realized man (zhen ren), one who has transcended the polarity of opposites and is awakened to the significance of the Dao underlying all reality. The zhen ren acts in a natural (ziran) manner, manifesting the doctrine of non-action or wu wei. Contrary to the absence of action, wu wei is action that is unforced, harmonious, and informed with virtue. By cultivating harmony, the mind of the Daoist sage moves spontaneously, and his actions are unpremeditated.

The *Daode Jing* and the *Zhuangzi* are the two key texts of philosophical Daoism. They cover a wide variety of subjects, from the most mundane aspects of human behavior to profound metaphysical speculation. It is significant that even with the later evolution of a complex Daoist religious pantheon, alchemy, the search for immortality, and the proliferation of Daoist sects, these texts— particularly the *Daode Jing*—continued to function as the fundamental documents on which all subsequent Daoist thought was based.

During the third and second centuries BC, several strands of Daoist philosophical thought and mystical practice began to congeal into a unified system. Among these originally separate currents was the theory that all natural phenomena could be explained as the workings of two opposing forces or cosmic influences, known as Yin and Yang. In short, Yin represented dark, cold, and weakness; while Yang represented light, heat, and strength.[6] Yin and Yang also represented female and male, respectively. Among other natural phenomema, the cycle of the seasons was explained as the reflection on an earthly scale of the cosmic fluctuations of Yin and Yang: in winter Yin was at its height, in summer, Yang.

A second theory adopted by early Daoists involved the Five Elements, or Wu xing. This theory was attributed in Sima Qian's *Records of the Historian (Shi Ji)* of the second century BC to the philosopher Zou Yan (ca. 325 BC).[7] The five elements are wood, metal, fire, water, and earth. Like Yin and Yang, these interact in repeating cycles, and an understanding of their interaction could also explain real phenomena. By the Han dynasty (206 BC-AD 220) this theory had come to be applied to dynastic succession. The Zhou dynasty (ca. 1050-256 BC), symbolized by fire, was thus succeeded by the short-lived but powerful Qin dynasty (221-207 BC), symbolized by water. The Han dynasty in turn adopted as its element earth, which according to the Five Elements theory overcame water.

A third current that developed into a major aspect of Daoist thought appeared at about the same time. This was the search for immortality. It was believed that certain herbs and drugs, when properly prepared and ingested, conferred life without end. These plants and minerals were most often found on mountains, which to Daoists were sacred places. The worship of mountains in China originated in prehistoric times, but by the end of the Bronze Age it was codified into a coherent system. Mountains, and the rocks from which they were made, were seen as crystallizations of primordial energies.[8] An important concept to emerge was the idea of the mountainous islands of the immortals, located off the eastern coast of China (Figure II). The best-known were Penglai, Fanghu, and Yingzhou. There the serious adept could find the plants and minerals that conferred immortality.

The search for these islands became a preoccupation of royalty. Among the earliest to send ships in search of Penglai was Duke Wei of Qi (r. 357-320 BC), whose domain, located in modern Shandong Province along China's northeast coast, was ideally situated for naval expeditions. During the Qin dynasty, the tyrant Shihuangdi (d. 210 BC) sent boats full of virgins under the direction of the Daoist magician Xu Fu into the eastern sea in search of Penglai, but none returned.[9]

Figure III. *The Great Lord of Fate*, detail from *The Nine Songs*. Handscroll, ink on paper. Zhang Wu, fourteenth century, Yuan dynasty. CMA 59.138.

The development of Daoism was given a powerful impetus during the early Han dynasty by the patronage of several emperors and their consorts. The founder of the Han, Liu Bang, was himself said to have been assisted in his campaigns by the Daoist Zhang Liang, who was personally instructed in the secrets of military strategy by an immortal. Emperor Wendi (r. 179-157 BC), his consort Empress Dou, and his son Jingdi (r. 156-141 BC) were followers of the Daoist philosophy as expounded in the *Daode Jing*.[10] One of the key Daoist philosophers of the period was a nephew of Jingdi named Liu An (ca. 179-122 BC), at whose court the book entitled *Huainanzi* was compiled. It is an important record of contemporary Daoist ideas regarding the natural world and human existence.[11]

Early imperial patronage of Daoism reached its height under the Han Emperor Wudi (r. 140-87 BC). Obsessed with becoming an immortal, Wudi invited many magicians (fangshi) to court. The most influential came from the region of the old state of Qi in Shandong and brought with them recipes for the elixirs of immortality. The fangshi are credited with blending ancient forms of sorcery with the cult of Laozi and techniques of longevity (chang sheng, literally: extended life).[12] Among the most influential of the fangshi was Li Shaojun, who convinced Wudi to subsidize experiments in which cinnabar was transmuted into gold. By using ritual vessels made of the resulting gold, Li claimed that the emperor would be able to see and communicate with immortals.[13] Another aspect of Li Shaojun's practice involved special breathing and meditation exercises designed to purge one's body and mind of obstacles to union with the Dao. Unfortunately, Li Shaojun died before enabling Wudi to become an immortal.

During this time the concept of the immortal, or xian, was codified. Xian could be found in mountains as well as in higher, more mystical realms. The idea that a human, using the proper means, could become an immortal spread widely in the centuries following the early Han. Gradually a mystical Daoist hierarchy emerged in which immortals functioned as officials in a celestial bureaucracy serving even higher and more remote Daoist gods. By becoming an immortal, one would attain a position in this bureaucracy of spirits.

The higher gods included the Yellow Emperor (Huang Di), the Queen Mother of the West (Xiwangmu), the Supreme Unity (Tai Yi), and the Lord of Fate (Siming). Of these deities Siming was probably the oldest, as he appears in inscriptions on ritual bronzes of the sixth century BC and was one the leading deities of the shamanistic *Nine Songs* (Figure III) of the state of Chu in the late Warring States Period (fifth-third century BC).[14] Siming was later identified with the popular Stove or Kitchen God, while Tai Yi came to be associated with the Pole Star. The Queen Mother of the West, the goddess Xiwangmu, began to be worshipped widely during the Han dynasty.[15] She was believed to rule over a paradise in the far west and to have access to the secrets of longevity and immortality. Xiwangmu was often depicted wearing a crown and accompanied by her attendants, the Jade Maidens (Yu nü). By the year AD 165, Laozi himself was officially deified and was known thereafter as the Supreme Ultimate Lord Lao (Taishang Laojun).[16]

3

The immortals, or xian, took on many of the attributes of the zhen ren of earlier times.[17] It is astonishing that this happened since the quest for immortality (as opposed to longevity) is ridiculed in the *Zhuangzi* and is never even mentioned in the *Daode Jing*. Regardless, these early texts continued to be revered as the primary sources of Daoist philosophy.

The early alchemist Li Shaojun's use of cinnabar (dan) in the search for immortality is significant, for this mineral continued to be a primary ingredient of many later elixirs. There is no doubt that cinnabar (mercuric sulphide) had for centuries been regarded as a sacred mineral. It appears in royal burials as early as the Shang dynasty (sixteenth-eleventh century BC) and is often seen encrusted in the grooves carved into Chinese jades of the Bronze Age.[18] Magical properties were also associated with jade, which had been worked in China since Neolithic times.

The association between jade and immortality is spectacularly illustrated by the jade burial suits excavated in 1968 from the early Han tomb of the imperial prince Liu Sheng and his wife Dou Wan at Mancheng, Hebei Province.[19] The encasement of the corpse with jade (or, more economically, the plugging of the bodily orifices with pieces of jade) was believed to prevent the deterioration of the part of the soul (the po) that remained with the body after death. The other part of the soul (the hun) was believed to rise to a higher plane after death.

At least four principal concepts of the afterworld were current during the Han dynasty. These were the island mountains such as Penglai in the eastern sea, the paradise in the Kunlun Mountains ruled by Xiwangmu, the nether world of the Yellow Springs, and the more nebulous but no less compelling concept of the Dao—the "structure of being that underlies the universe."[20]

While the ethereal hun was worshipped in the deceased's ancestral shrine, the happiness of the material soul, or po, was ensured by providing for its existence in the afterlife. Thus originated the elaborate burials of the Bronze Age and later times, in which clothing, food, religious texts, diagrams of the nether world, sculpted models of musicians, servants, warriors, and guardians, works of art, and quotidian objects were interred with the corpse. It is in the burials of the Han dynasty that we see some of the earliest appearances in art of the immortals (xian) inhabiting mountainous paradises [9-10].

In the second century AD, during the collapse of the Han, major developments occurred that had a lasting impact on Daoism. The first was the appearance of a Daoist visionary named Yu Ji in Langye, Shandong. Yu produced a text that he claimed was dictated to him by spirits—the *Book of Pure Commands of the Great Peace.*[21] According to this and the slightly later *Classic of the Great Peace (Taiping Jing)*, mankind had, since high antiquity, become increasingly divorced from the Dao.[22] Both books taught that mankind could return to state of harmony only through the cultivation and purification of the spirit, the aim being to transcend the "red dust" of the material world. The adoption of the Way of the Great Peace (Taiping dao) and its spiritual exercises promised to lead to longevity and even immortality.

A second important development was the appearance of a sect called the Way of the Celestial Master (Tianshi dao), also known as the Way of the Five Bushels of Rice (Wu dou mi dao). The founder of this sect was Zhang Daoling, who was born in Jiangsu Province. Eventually he settled in Sichuan, where he was visited by the deified spirit of Laozi (see [2]). The members of his sect paid a regular tribute of five bushels of rice. Their rituals, although ultimately based on the teachings of the *Daode Jing*, were focused on faith healing and other miracles, and stressed good works. Zhang Daoling's power derived from his knowledge of the Twenty-Four Auspicious Alliance Registers of higher spirits, which he could summon on one's behalf in a higher realm.[23] The sect had an enormous following among the populace in southern China, and lasted well into the Six Dynasties Period (third-sixth century AD). The leaders of the sect became known as Celestial Masters (Tian shi).

The widespread influence of the Celestial Master sect is illustrated by the creation of an independent theocratic Daoist state in Sichuan under Zhang Daoling's grandson Zhang Lu in the early third century AD, and the adherence to this sect of many of the leading literati of the early Six Dynasties Period, including the painter Gu Kaizhi (ca. 344-ca. 406) and the family of the "Sage of Calligraphy," Wang Xizhi (307-365).[24] The earliest known pictorial depiction of Zhang Daoling and his disciples, for example, was painted by Gu Kaizhi and is discussed in his essay, "Painting the Cloud Terrace Mountain."[25] Wang Xizhi inscribed many Daoist texts with his inimitable brush and, on one occasion, traded a copy of the *Classic of the Yellow Court (Huangting Jing)* for some geese owned by a Daoist priest.[26] The influence of Zhang Daoling was widespread in the early Six Dynasties Period, and the later Celestial Masters of the Orthodox Unity (Zhengyi) sect in the Song, Yuan, Ming, and Qing dynasties traced their origins back to him.

A third development of the late Han was the Yellow Turban Revolt, led by a Daoist named Zhang Jue. This popular uprising against the Han ruling house took place in AD 184. The Daoist concepts used by the Yellow Turbans were essentially those of Yu Ji. These men believed that upon overturning the Han, a new era of "Great Peace" would ensue. The revolt was put down by the Han government, however, and from this time on Daoism remained primarily a religious movement with relatively few political ambitions:

The rebellion of the Yellow Turbans in the eastern provinces, led by Zhang Jue in AD 184 and tirelessly suppressed by the Later Han government through the next two decades, left behind many communities [in following centuries] *which, though no longer posing a powerful political threat, continued to follow the original religious practices of the Way of Great Peace, including prayer and fasting, group confessions to obtain healing, group recitations of the* Daode Jing *and other sacred texts, and a quasi-military hierarchy of local and regional officers who became hereditary and were supported through regular contributions of rice and other commodities.*[27]

The downfall of the Han dynasty in AD 220 and the political and social unrest accompanying the successive invasions of northern China by nomadic barbarians led to an even greater interest in Daoism in both the north and the south. During the Six Dynasties Period, Daoism split into numerous sects and there emerged a widespread interest in alchemy. The Way of the Great Peace (Taiping Dao) in central and eastern China continued as an important sect that emerged from the following of the late Han Daoist leaders Yu Ji and Zhang Jue. The central text of this sect was the *Taiping Jing*, which promised the return of a golden age if humanity purified itself. Both the leading Daoist sects and the preeminent alchemists of the late Han period had stressed the importance of cultivating virtue, for a clear conscience was a prerequisite of salvation and immortality. The majority of the leading Daoist sects incorporated breathing and meditation exercises in their disciplines. The function of these techniques was to circulate the Vital Breaths, through which the adept became purified. The human body was conceived as containing many vital centers inhabited by deities whose celestial counterparts lived in the stars. With the proper techniques, a disciplined practitioner could refine and direct his spiritual energies (qi) toward transcendence, resulting in the creation within his body of a "Divine Embryo" which existed like a child in harmony with the Dao and which ascended to heaven upon his death.[28]

At the heart of the leading alchemical theories and practices of the Six Dynasties Period were the elixirs of immortality. The most powerful of these contained cinnabar, a toxic poison. The earliest alchemical text that specifically mentioned the use of cinnabar in an elixir was the late Han Daoist Wei Boyang's *The Threefold Unity (Cantong ji)* of ca. AD 140.[29] A potent elixir would be prepared in a crucible through many firing cycles. One reads, for example, of a Cyclically Transformed Elixir of Immortality (huan dan) which contained lead and mercury, symbolized in alchemical terminology by the tiger and dragon.

Similar recipes appear in the *Baopuzi* by Ge Hong (AD 283-340), one of the most important Daoist philosophers and alchemists of the Six Dynasties Period. The *Baopuzi* provides a rich source of contemporary material for our understanding of many Daoist beliefs of this time.[30] A recipe for an elixir called Flowers of Cinnabar reads as follows:

Figure IV. *Immortal Riding a Dragon.* Hanging scroll, ink on silk. Ma Yuan, early thirteenth century, Southern Song dynasty. National Palace Museum, Taipei.

6

It is begun by preparing some "tin oxide" (a preparation of tin and mercury, used to coat the crucibles inside and out ...). From several dozen pounds each of realgar solution, kalanite solution, Turkestan salt, lake salt, arsenolite, oyster shells, red bole, soapstone, and white lead, prepare Six-One cement, with which to cover both clay crucibles inside and out. The crucibles are then dried slowly in the sun for ten days. The elixir will be ready after being fired for thirty-six days, and if you take it for seven days you will become an immortal.[31]

Besides cinnabar and the minerals listed above, Ge Hong also used gold, malachite, sulphur, mica, saltpeter, and orpiment in his elixirs. Citing a now-lost text, Ge Hong commented on the necessity of taking elixirs if one wanted to become an immortal:

We read in the Huangdi jiuding shendan jing [The classic of the Yellow Emperor's nine-crucible divine elixir] *that Huangdi rose into the sky and became an immortal after taking this elixir. It adds that by merely doing the breathing exercises and calisthenics and taking herbal medicines, one may extend one's years but cannot prevent ultimate death. Taking the divine elixir, however, will produce an interminable longevity and make one coeval with sky and earth; it lets one travel up and down in Paradise, riding clouds and driving dragons.[32]*

The image of the zhen ren or xian riding a dragon had existed for centuries by the time that Ge Hong wrote the *Baopuzi*. One of the earliest known Chinese paintings on silk, excavated in 1973 from a tomb near Changsha, Hunan Province, dating to the Warring States Period (fifth-third centuries BC), depicts a man riding a dragon.[33] This image appears again many centuries after Ge Hong in the thirteenth-century court artist Ma Yuan's *Immortal Riding a Dragon* now in the National Palace Museum, Taipei (Figure IV).[34] By riding the dragon the adept demonstrated the transcendence of his earth-bound existence. Concurrently, the dragon became a symbol of the Dao itself, as well as the rejuvenating Yang force, as it rose out of the ocean in spring, bringing water to the earth (Figure V).[35]

It is noteworthy that Ge Hong admonished the adept who sought immortality not to neglect the development of his own moral virtue before attempting such a risky journey into the beyond. In the following passage Ge reveals his grounding in traditional Confucianism:

Those wishing to seek immortality should think of loyalty, filial piety, friendliness, obedience, the human ideal, and trustworthiness as basic. If they do not perform meritorious actions but solely pursue the esoteric techniques, they will never attain Extended Life.[36]

Elsewhere, Ge Hong echoes the traditional Daoist belief expressed in the *Daode Jing*, that aspects of the phenomenal world are transitory, and therefore destructive to one's spiritual development if one takes too great in interest in them:

Figure V. *Dragon Emerging from the Waves.* Hanging scroll, ink on paper. Li Yi, Ming dynasty. Tokiwayama Bunko, Kamakura.

Distinguishing the five notes, the eight instruments, and the various musical modes wears away our hearing. Ornamentation with all its variety and beauty with its brilliance harms our eyesight. Festive gatherings, leisure, indulgence, and drinking throw our very natures into disorder. Lovely faces, fair skins artfully painted, erode our very lives. It is only with the Mystery that is Dao that there can be permanence.[37]

In the early sixth century AD, the other great alchemist of the Six Dynasties Period, Tao Hongjing (456-536), created a major center of Daoist study on Mao Shan near the southern capital of Nanjing.[38] Patronized by the Liang dynasty Emperor Wudi (r. 502-549), Tao Hongjing was famous both as a Daoist practitioner and as a compiler and editor of the basic texts associated with the Mao Shan sect of Daoism and its mystical revelations. The Mao Shan, or Great Clarity (Shangqing), sect used the difficult *Classic of the Yellow Court (Huangting Jing)* as its primary guide to meditation.[39] Among Tao's best-known writings are his critical notes on the *Shen Nong Pharmacopoeia,* the *Concealed Instructions for Ascent to Perfection,* and the *Declarations of the Perfected.*[40] The latter consisted of the fragments of the original Mao Shan revelations that Tao Hongjing compiled from a confusing mass of authentic manuscripts and early forgeries through his connoisseurship of the calligraphy of the Mao Shan patriarchs Yang Xi (b. 330) and his disciples Xu Mi (303-373) and Xu Hui (341-ca.370). The scholastic bent of Tao Hongjing's Daoism was typical of the Mao Shan sect which, as Michael Saso has shown, "was in its beginnings an order founded for and by the highest literati class in the courts of the southern kingdoms" of the Six Dynasties Period.[41]

The elixirs described by Tao Hongjing were guaranteed to transform one into an immortal, and their astonishing properties are suggested by their resonant names, which include Efflorescence of Langgan, Powder of Liquified Gold, Dragon Foetus, Jade Essence, Gold Elixir, and the Nine-times Cycled.[42] These alchemical agents were revealed by the perfected beings of the heaven of Shangqing to the fourth-century Daoist Yang Xi in a text known as the *Sword Scripture (Jian Jing).* As Strickmann has demonstrated in his study of Tao Hongjing's alchemy, it is clear that the ingestion of these toxic elixirs meant certain death (and, presumably, rebirth in paradise as an immortal) for the practitioner:

Anyone undertaking the preparation of this powder ... must certainly have known what laid in store for him when the work was completed. Within this context, the prospective alchemist must have been strongly motivated by faith and sustained by a firm confidence in his posthumous destiny. In effect, he would be committing suicide by consecrated means.[43]

Figure VI. *Stele with Taishang Laojun.* Stone. Northern Zhou dynasty, dated AD 567. Courtesy of the Freer Gallery of Art, Smithsonian Institution, Washington, D.C.

8

The Mao Shan sect, of which Tao Hongjing was the leading spokesman, derived many of its basic beliefs from the remnants of the first Celestial Master sect of the late Han, and continued to be the major school of Daoism in the Tang dynasty (618-906).

At several points during the Six Dynasties Period debates were held at imperial courts between Buddhists and Daoists, and occasionally one group or the other was humiliated and suffered persecution.[44] For a brief period during the Northern Wei dynasty, for example, the Daoist Gou Qianzhi convinced the emperor Tai Wudi (r. 424-452) to establish Daoism as the state religion, and a severe persecution of Buddhism ensued for six years after 446.[45] Thoroughly entranced by Daoist magic, Tai Wudi wished to become an immortal. Fortunately the proscription of Buddhism came to an end with his death. Aside from the Northern Wei, only the short-lived Northern Zhou dynasty (557-581) utilized strict Daoist rites as its official ceremonial functions.[46] It was also during the Northern Zhou and succeeding Sui dynasties that many Daoist stone stelae were carved in honor of the deified Laozi, consciously borrowing a format from contemporary Buddhist sculpture (Figure VI).[47]

Imperial patronage of Daoism continued during the Tang dynasty and was to one extent linked to the fact that the original surname of Laozi and the Tang imperial family was the same (Li). The Tang emperor Gaozong (r. 650-683) conferred a new title on Laozi: "Supreme Emperor of the Mystic Origin." The Tang witnessed the spread of Daoist monasteries (guan) throughout China, which competed for novices with Buddhist temples. The Daoist church of this period became increasingly organized and issued certificates of ordination to priests, monks, and nuns. During the Tang, Daoist rituals became more public and elaborate in their orientation. The rites of the Lingbao sect, traditionally established in the Six Dynasties Period by Ge Xuan and Ge Hong, focused on spirit-summoning, the jiao ceremony of cosmic renewal, and the zhai rites for the dead, and were gradually adopted by other Daoist sects and the imperial court.[48]

The Tang Emperor Xuanzong (Minghuang) of the early eighth century was so devoted to Daoism that he ordered that every city in China should have a Daoist temple, and himself took a lay degree from the master Sima Chengzhen in 721.[49] Twenty years later the *Daode Jing* and other Daoist texts were officially sanctioned as literary and religious classics, and were inscribed on stone tablets. The ecumenical nature of Daoism in the Tang is reflected in the fact that Sima Chengzhen was at once conversant with the beliefs and liturgy of the Mao Shan, Celestial Master, and Lingbao sects.[50]

Following the An Lushan rebellion of 755-756, the Tang dynasty began a long decline, and during the ninth century several emperors became fixated on the search for immortality. Included among them were Xianzong (r. 805-820), Muzong (r. 820-824), Wuzong (r. 840-846), and Xuanzong (r. 847-859). All died from overdoses of cinnabar.[51] Of these emperors, Wuzong was the most notorious, for he instigated the harshest proscription of Buddhism in Chinese history under the influence of his Daoist alchemists and priests.

Daoism continued to be patronized by the emperors of the Song dynasty (960-1279), particularly Zhenzong (r. 998-1020) and Huizong (r. 1101-1126). The latter is well-known to art historians as a refined aesthete and a brilliant painter. Huizong, who considered himself a reincarnation of the Yellow Emperor, commissioned the first printed edition of the Daoist Cannon (*Daocang*) in ca. 1117-1120.[52]

By the end of the Song two principal sects of Daoism had emerged that lasted into the twentieth century. The first was the Complete Realization (Quanzhen) sect. It was founded by Wang Zhe (1112-1170), a native of Shaanxi Province who was active under the Jin dynasty (1115-1234) in north China, coeval with the Southern Song dynasty. The emphasis of the Quanzhen sect

Figure VII. *The Three Religions (Laozi, Confucius, and Buddha).* Hanging scroll, ink on silk. Anonymous, Ming dynasty. Nelson-Atkins Museum, Kansas City.

Figure VIII. *Laozi in the Guise of the Buddha.* Hanging scroll, ink and colors on silk. Anonymous, Ming dynasty. Hatakeyama Museum, Tokyo.

was on asceticism and meditation, the ultimate aim of which was to purify an individual's inner self. Quanzhen priests were therefore celibate, and their lives focused on monastic discipline.[53] This sect was deeply influenced by both neo-Confucian philosophy and Chan (Zen) Buddhism. Wang Zhe's emphasis on teachings that resembled those of Confucianism and Buddhism reflects the growing impact of the Three Religions (Sanjiao) philosophy, which in its most basic form stated that Confucianism, Buddhism, and Daoism were different paths to the same truth (Figure VII).[54] Thus, among the texts used in Wang Zhe's teachings were the *Classic of Filial Piety (Xiao Jing),* the Buddhist *Heart Sūtra,* and the *Daode Jing.* By the mid-thirteenth century, the center of the Quanzhen sect was the White Cloud Monastery (Baiyun guan) in the western suburbs of Beijing.[55]

The syncreticism reflected in Wang Zhe's teaching is vividly illustrated in an anonymous Ming dynasty (fifteenth century) painting in the Hatakeyama Museum, Tokyo (Figure VIII).[56] The subject is similar to that shown in Shang Xi's *Laozi Encountering Yin Xi at the Han'gu Pass* (Figure I), which depicts Laozi transmitting the text of the *Daode Jing* to the gatekeeper Yin Xi as the sage left China for the western regions of Central Asia. In the Hatakeyama painting, however, Laozi appears on an ox in the guise of the Buddha. This peculiar iconography is undoubtedly a late manifestation of the theories that emerged out of the Buddhist-Daoist debates of the Six Dynasties Period, claiming that "the Buddha was either a convert to or a manifestation of Laozi who had gone to India to convert the barbarians."[57] In the Six Dynasties Period one function of such a claim was to show that Buddhism was essentially the same thing as Daoism, and that the latter had existed well before the former. By the early Ming dynasty, an image such as that seen in the Hatakeyama painting reflected a similar belief, although one in which the two religions were seen not as mutually antagonistic but as different aspects of the same higher reality.

The second important sect of the Song dynasty and later periods was known as Orthodox Unity (Zhengyi). Centered at Longhu Shan, Jiangxi Province, in southern China, the Zhengyi sect traced its lineage back to Zhang Daoling, the first Celestial Master of the late Han dynasty. The later Celestial Masters of this sect all had the surname Zhang, and from the time of Khubilai Khan onwards (late thirteenth century) were recognized as the legitimate leaders of the sect by the emperors of the Yuan, Ming, and Qing dynasties. As Saso has shown, the imperial patronage of the Zhengyi sect ensured its paramount influence over the evolution of the Daoist liturgy and ritual.[58] The variations in priests' robes highlight the differences between the northern Quanzhen and southern Zhengyi sects:

In general, daoshi [Daoist priests] of the Quanzhen sect emphasize individual practice. They roam the mountains in search of medicinal herbs. To allow for their practice of austerity, their robes are light and simple. Daoshi belonging to the Way of the Celestial Masters [the Zhengyi sect] emphasize devotional activities. They devote much of their time to magical incantations, prayers, and festivals. Their robes are correspondingly elaborate.[59]

Among the two best-known Daoist writers of the Song period were Zhang Boduan (987-1082) and Bai Yuchan (1134-1220). Zhang, who like the Six Dynasties Period alchemist Ge Hong received a classical Confucian education as a young man, developed a keen interest in Daoist meditation and in alchemy.[60] His *Four Hundred Words on the Gold-Cinnabar Elixir* is a guidebook to union with the Dao written in the now-familiar metaphorical language of alchemy. Zhang was also the author of the *Essay on Awakening to Reality (Wuzhen bian),* a major text of later Daoist philosophy.[61]

Bai Yuchan was the leading Daoist philosopher of the Southern Song dynasty (1127-1368), and he too mastered the teachings of several Daoist sects. Among his significant achievements was the consolidation of the popular Thunder Magic rituals into orthodox Daoist practice. The Thunder Magic sect originated during the Tang dynasty, and its rituals were primarily exorcistic in nature and heavily influenced by the rites of Vajrayana or Tantric Buddhism. Emperor Huizong was a great patron of Thunder Magic, and court rituals honoring the nominal founder of the sect, Xu Xun (240-374), were instituted in AD 1112.[62]

In the Song dynasty one finds the earliest worship of the Eight Immortals, a popular group of transcendents with magical powers who figure prominently in the visual arts of the Yuan and later dynasties (Figures IX, XI).[63] The majority of the Eight Immortals emanate from the Tang dynasty and present a strik-

Figure IX. *Vase with the Eight Immortals.* Longquan Celadon ware. Fourteenth century, Yuan dynasty. Philadelphia Museum of Art.

Figure XIa. *Lü Dongbin* (after *Sancai tuhui,* 1607).

Figure XIb. *Zhang Guolao* (after *Sancai tuhui,* 1607).

Figure XIc. *Zhongli Quan* (after *Sancai tuhui,* 1607).

Figure XId. *Li Tieguai* (after *Sancai tuhui,* 1607).

a

b

c

d

Figure X. *Lü Dongbin Receiving the Secrets of Daoism from Zhongli Quan.* Hanging scroll, ink and colors on silk. Anonymous, fourteenth century, Yuan dynasty. MOA Museum, Atami.

Figure XIe. *Han Xiangzi* (after *Sancai tuhui*, 1607).

Figure XIf. *Cao Guoqiu* (after *Sancai tuhui*, 1607).

Figure XIg. *Lan Caihe* (after *Sancai tuhui*, 1607).

Figure XIh. *He Xian'gu* (after *Sancai tuhui*, 1607).

ing cross-section of society. Associated with the Eight Immortals were many supernatural tales, recounting their transcendence to immortality and their miraculous powers. One of the best-known of the Eight Immortals was Lü Dongbin, who learned the secrets of Daoism from the immortal Zhongli Quan (another of the Eight) after experiencing an entire lifetime of official success and failure in a dream (Figure X).[64] Worshipped as a patron saint of the northern Quanzhen sect of Daoism, Lü is depicted along with the other seven of the Eight Immortals in the fourteenth-century wall paintings at the Yongle Gong in Ruicheng, Shanxi Province, the earliest surviving Quanzhen temple.[65] Venerated as a great poet and swordsman, Lü is usually depicted with a sword strapped to his back (Figure XIa).

The use of such attributes assists in the identification of the Eight Immortals. Thus, Zhang Guolao is often shown with his mule (which he could fold up and put in a bag; see Figure XIb), Zhongli Quan with a fan (Figure XIc, [6]), Li Tieguai (who appropriated the body of a crippled beggar after returning from an astral journey to find that his own moribund body had been cremated) with an iron crutch (Figure XId, [14]), Han Xiangxi (nephew of the Tang poet Han Yu) with a flute or a "fish-drum" (Figure XIe), Cao Guoqiu (a tenth-century aristocrat and patron deity of actors) with a fly-whisk or a pair of castanets (Figure XIf), Lan Caihe with a percussion instrument or jieban (Figure XIg), and the female immortal He Xian'gu with a basket of magic mushrooms or a lotus flower (Figure XIh, [15]).

The Mongol emperors of the Yuan dynasty (1279-1368) were also patrons of Daoism (as well as, it should be noted, of Buddhism). In the thirteenth century Genghis Khan summoned the Daoist alchemist Changchun to his capital in Central Asia, and Genghis' grandson Khubilai Khan successively recognized both Li Zhichang of the Quanzhen sect and the Celestial Master Zhang Zong-yan of the Zhengyi sect as legitimate Daoist patriarchs.[66] Daoist priests enjoyed

11

e

f

g

h

12

a   b

Figures XIIa-b. *Li Tieguai and Liu Haichan.* Pair of hanging scrolls, ink and colors on silk. Yan Hui, late thirteenth-early fourteenth century, Yuan dynasty. Chion-in, Kyoto.

a resurgence of political influence under the Mongols, who were impressed by their magical and healing powers.

Several of the leading painters of the Yuan dynasty were strongly influenced by Daoism. One of the best-known was Huang Gongwang (1269-1354), who worked as a professional diviner after leaving a minor bureaucratic post and being imprisoned. Recent study of his masterpiece, *Dwelling in the Fuchun Mountains*, suggests the direct impact of Daoist conceptions of geomancy, or the study of auspicious geological forms, in his work.[67] Another Yuan painter, Yan Hui, was famous for his figural murals in Daoist temples, as well as for his handscrolls and hanging scrolls.[68] Among his surviving works are a depiction of the Tang dynasty demon queller Zhong Kui with a procession of demons [7] and a pair of hanging scrolls in the Chion-in, Kyoto, depicting the immortals Li Tieguai (one of the Eight Immortals) and Liu Haichan (Figures XIIa-b).[69] The latter is often equated with an historical personage who lived in the early tenth century, credited with founding a southern branch of the Quanzhen sect.[70] He is shown with his emblem, the three-legged toad, which can transport him anywhere in the universe. During the Yuan and Ming dynasties, Li Tieguai and Liu Haichan were often depicted as a pair, and sometimes shown with the Tang dynasty Chan Buddhist eccentrics Hanshan and Shide (Figures XIIIa-d).[71] This was yet another manifestation of the syncreticism in later Chinese religion, in which Buddhist and Daoist (as well as Confucian) deities were worshipped together.

During the Ming dynasty (1368-1644) the Daoist canon (*Daocang*) was published in the form in which it exists today, consisting of over a thousand volumes. At the same time, the number of monastic centers authorized to ordain priests was limited by the government, leading to a greater degree of orthodoxy within religious Daoism.[72] Although the majority of the Ming emperors patronized both Buddhism and Daoism, the Jiajing emperor (r. 1522-1566)

13

Figures XIIIa-d. *Li Tieguai, Liu Haichan, Hanshan, and Shide.* Set of four hanging scrolls, ink and colors on silk. Liu Jun, fifteenth century, Ming dynasty. Tokyo National Museum.

a

b

c

d

14

Figure XIV. *Vase with Daoist Motifs.* Blue-and-white porcelain. Mark and period of Jiajing (1522-1566). Ming dynasty. National Palace Museum, Taipei.

was fanatical in his devotion to Daoism. Like Han Wudi, he desperately sought immortality.[73] He summoned alchemists to the Forbidden City in Beijing and in 1544 made a Daoist priest Secretary of the Board of Rites. The depletion of the imperial treasury stemming from the emperor's fascination with elixirs and Daoist ceremonies contributed to the initial decline of the political fortunes of the Ming dynasty. The pronounced imperial patronage of Daoism in this period is reflected in the blue-and-white porcelains made for the court, which are often decorated with dragons, cranes, hares, mushrooms, auspicious constellations, and transcendents—all symbols of longevity and immortality (Figure XIV).[74]

The orthodox sects of the Ming dynasty continued in an unbroken tradition through the Manchu-dominated Qing dynasty (1644-1911) and still exist today. Daoist priests remain active in Taiwan and Hong Kong, and may yet appear in greater numbers in the People's Republic of China, where the religious practices of Daoism have until recently suffered from the enforcement of the Marxist doctrine. Daoism is so ingrained in almost all aspects of traditional Chinese thought, however, that its impact will always be visible.

The works of art in this exhibition illustrate only a small aspect of the influence of Daoism in Chinese art. The earliest are objects designed for burial in tombs of the Han dynasty, and they are decorated with symbols, animals, and figures relating directly to the desire for rebirth in a Daoist paradise. Among them are some of the earliest depictions of immortals in Chinese art [9, 10]. The bulk of the material, however, dates to the Song, Yuan, Ming, and Qing dynasties (tenth-nineteenth centuries AD). Included are illustrations of the early sages of Daoism [1, 2], immortals [6, 14, 15, 22], alchemists [4], and popular deities such as Xiwangmu [12, 17], Shoulao [13], and the Three Stars [18]. Common Daoist symbolism represented in the exhibition include the peaches and mushrooms of immortality [17, 24, 25], mountains [21], paradises [5, 8, 16], and auspicious imperial regalia [23]. This selective group suggests the broad impact of Daoist philosophy and religion in the arts of China over the last two millennia.

NOTES

1. As Burton Watson has shown in his *Early Chinese Literature* (New York: Columbia University Press, 1962): "Scholars now agree that the biographical accounts of Lao Dan [Laozi] are no more than a jumble of confused legends..." (p. 157). See [1]. It is likely, as Arthur Waley points out in *The Way and Its Power: A Study of the Tao Te Ching and Its Place in Chinese Thought* (New York: Grove Press, 1958), pp. 106-108, that the author of the *Daode Jing* was a composite figure.

2. For an excellent translation of this text, see Waley, *The Way and Its Power*. On the book's original function, see his introduction, pp. 17-100.

3. Ibid., p. 187 (*Daode Jing*, chap. 35).

4. Ibid., p. 160.

5. For a discussion and translation of the *Zhuangzi*, see Burton Watson, trans., *The Complete Works of Chuang Tzu* (New York: Columbia University Press, 1968).

6. Waley, *The Way and Its Power*, p. 110.

7. On Zou Yan and the Five Elements theory, see Fung Yu-lan, *A Short History of Chinese Philosophy* (New York: The MacMillan Co., 1948), pp. 135-138; for a translation of Sima Qian's account of Zou Yan in the *Shi Ji*, see Szuma Chien [Sima Qian], *Selections from Records of the Historian*, trans. Yang Hsien-yi and Gladys Yang (Beijing: Foreign Languages Press, 1979), p. 71.

8. See the discussion of rocks and energy in John Hay, *Kernels of Energy, Bones of Earth: The Rock in Chinese Art* (New York: China Institute, 1985), pp. 50-53.

9. On Duke Wei of Qi, see Holmes Welch, *Taoism: The Parting of the Way* (Boston: Beacon Press, 1957), p. 97 (hereafter cited as *Taoism*); on Qin Shihuangdi's search for the islands of the immortals, see Szuma Chien [Sima Qian], *Selections*, p. 173.

10. Michael Loewe, *Chinese Ideas of Life and Death* (London: George Allen and Unwin, 1982), pp. 43, 182; also Welch, *Taoism*, pp. 104-105.

11. Watson, *Early Chinese Literature*, pp. 189-191.

12. Michael Saso, *The Teachings of Taoist Master Chuang* (New Haven and London: Yale University Press, 1978), pp. 19-20 (hereafter cited as *Teachings*); see also Rolf Stein, "Religious Taoism and Popular Religion from the Second to Seventh Centuries," in Holmes Welch and Anna Seidel, eds., *Facets of Taoism: Essays in Chinese Religion* (New Haven and London: Yale University Press, 1979), p. 80 (hereafter cited as Welch and Seidel, eds., *Facets*).

13. Welch, *Taoism*, pp. 99-102.

14. Ibid., p. 100, and Stein, "Religious Taoism," pp. 76-79.

15. On Xiwangmu, see [12].

16. Arthur Pontynen, "The Deification of Laozi in Chinese History and Art," *Oriental Art*, 26, no. 2 (Summer 1980), 193.

17. Welch, *Taoism*, p. 92.

18. Kwang-chih Chang, *The Archaeology of Ancient China*, 3rd ed. (New Haven and London: Yale University Press, 1979), p. 222.

19. William Watson, *The Chinese Exhibition* (London: Times Newspapers, 1974), no. 139.

20. Loewe, *Chinese Ideas*, pp. 27-28.

21. Saso, *Teachings*, pp. 24-25.

22. Max Kaltenmark, "The Ideology of the *T'ai-p'ing Ching*," in Holmes and Seidel, eds., *Facets*, p. 22.

23. Saso, *Teachings*, p. 17.

24. The character *zhi* at the end of an individual's first name indicated adherence to the Way of the Celestial Master. It is noteworthy that cinnabar pills have been excavated from the tomb of a female relative of Wang Xizhi (Stein, "Religious Taoism," p. 55, n. 7 [citing *Wenwu*, 1965, no. 10, p. 38]).

25. Yu Jianhua, *Zhongguo hualun leibian*, 2 vols. (1956; reprint Hong Kong: Zhonghua shuju, 1973), 1:581-582; translated in *Some T'ang and Pre-T'ang Texts on Chinese Painting*, trans. William Acker, 2 vols. (Leiden: H. Brill, 1954), vol. 1, pt. 2, pp. 73-82.

26. The anecdote is recounted in *Jinshu* (Dynastic history of the Jin), chap. 50; see Kwan S. Wong, *Masterpieces of Sung and Yüan Dynasty Calligraphy from the John M. Crawford, Jr., Collection* (New York: China Institute, 1981), no. 13, pp. 72-73.

27. Richard B. Mather, "K'ou Ch'ien-chih and the Taoist Theocracy at the Northern Wei Court, 425-451," in Welch and Seidel, eds., *Facets*, p. 105.

28. Kaltenmark, "Ideology of the *T'ai-p'ing Ching*," p. 43.

29. Nathan Sivin, *Chinese Alchemy: Preliminary Studies* (Cambridge, Mass.: Harvard University Press, 1968), pp. 36-40.

30. For a discussion of Ge Hong and a translation of his autobiography, see James Ware, *Alchemy and Religion in the China of AD 320: The Nei P'ien of Ko Hung* (Cambridge, Mass.: Massachusetts Institute of Technology Press, 1966), pp. 1-21.

31. Ibid., p. 76.

32. Ibid., p. 71.

33. *Kaogu*, 1973, no. 7, pp. 3-4. See also Hunan Provincial Museum, "Paintings on Silk from a Chu Tomb of the Warring States Period Found in Changsha," in *New Archaeological Finds in China* (Beijing: Foreign Languages Press, 1978), pp. 48-54.

34. Recorded in Zhang Zhao, et al., *Shiqu baoji* (1745; reprint Taipei: National Palace Museum, 1970), p. 1104.

35. Published in Suzuki Kei, *Chūgoku kaiga sōgo zuroku*, 5 vols. (Tokyo: Heibonsha, 1982), 4:no. JP1-006. Li Yi was a native of Fujian Province; his dates are unknown.

36. Translated in Ware, *Alchemy*, p. 66.

37. Translated in Ware, ibid., p. 29.

38. For an excellent study of Tao Hongjing, see Michel Strickmann, "On the Alchemy of T'ao Hung-ching," in Welch and Seidel, eds., *Facets*, pp. 123-192.

39. Saso, *Teachings*, p. 17.

40. Ibid., p. 43; Strickmann, "Alchemy of T'ao Hung-ching," p. 126.

41. Saso, *Teachings*, p. 38.

42. Strickmann, "Alchemy of T'ao Hung-ching," pp. 132-133.

43. Ibid., pp. 137-138.

44. On these debates, see Kenneth Ch'en, *Buddhism in China: A Historical Survey* (Princeton: Princeton University Press, 1964), pp. 184-194.

45. Mather, "K'ou Ch'ien-chih," pp. 104 ff.

46. Ibid., p. 119.

47. See Pontynen, "Deification of Laozi," fig. 4 (Freer Gallery of Art, Smithsonian Institution, access. no. Bishop 513.3).

48. Saso, *Teachings*, pp. 32, 43.

49. Welch, *Taoism*, p. 153.

50. Saso, *Teachings*, pp. 47-48.

51. Peng Yoke He, *Li, Qi and Shu* (Hong Kong: Hong Kong University Press, 1985), p. 184.

52. Strickmann, "Alchemy of T'ao Hung-ching," p. 158, n. 106. See also his article, "The Longest Taoist Scripture," *History of Religions*, 17, nos. 3-4 (February-March 1978), 331-354.

53. Saso, *Teachings*, p. 52.

54. Published in *Eight Dynasties of Chinese Painting: The Collections of the Nelson Gallery-Atkins Museum, Kansas City, and The Cleveland Museum of Art* (Cleveland, 1980), no. 153.

55. For an excellent discussion of daily life in this Quanzhen monastery in the twentieth century, see Yoshitoyo Yoshioka, "Taoist Monastic Life," in Welch and Seidel, eds., *Facets*, pp. 229-252.

56. Published in *Gendai dōshaku jinbutsuga* (Tokyo: Tokyo National Museum, 1975), no. 61.

57. Pontynen, "Deification of Laozi," p. 23.

58. Saso, *Teachings*, pp. 53.

59. Yoshioka, "Taoist Monastic Life," p. 238.

60. See Chang Po-tuan [Zhang Boduan], *The Inner Teachings of Taoism*, trans. Thomas Cleary (Boulder and London: Shambala, 1986), pp. xiv-xix.

61. Ibid., p. 4; see also Chao Yun-ts'ung and T. L. Davis, "Chang Po-tuan of T'ien T'ai, his *Wu Chen P'ien*," *Proceedings of the American Academy of Arts and Sciences*, 73, no. 5 (July 1939).

62. Saso, *Teachings*, p. 53. On Xu Xun, see [4].

63. The Longquan celadon vase is published in Sherman E. Lee and Wai-kam Ho, *Chinese Art under the Mongols: The Yüan Dynasty, 1279-1368* (Cleveland, 1968), no. 82.

64. See the biography of Lü Dongbin in Wang Shizhen, comp., *Liexian quanzhuan* (1598); reprinted in *Zhongguo gudai banhua congkan* (Shanghai: Wenwu chubanshe, 1961). The painting of Zhongli Quan and Lü Dongbin in the MOA Museum, Atami, is published in *Gendai dōshaku jinbutsuga*, no. 63.

65. Published in *Yongle gong* (Shanghai: Renmin meishu chubanshe, 1964), pl. 179. On the Yongle Gong, see Nancy Shatzman Steinhardt, et al., *Chinese Traditional Architecture* (New York: China Institute, 1984), pp. 133-137.

66. On Changchun, see Arthur Waley, *The Travels of an Alchemist* (London, 1931); on Khubilai Khan's patronage of Daoism see Welch, *Taoism*, pp. 154-155.

67. Alan John Hay, Huang Kung-wang's "Dwelling in the Fu-ch'un Mountains: Dimensions of a Landscape" (Ph.D. diss., Princeton University, 1978), pp. 274-277. For a study of another Yuan Daoist landscape painter, see Mary Gardner Neill, "Mountains of the Immortals: The Life and Painting of Fang Ts'ung-i" (Ph.D. diss., Yale University, 1981).

68. On Yan Hui, see James Cahill, *Hills Beyond a River: Chinese Painting of the Yüan Dynasty, 1279-1368* (New York and Tokyo: John Weatherhill, 1976), pp. 134, 151.

69. Published in Osvald Sirén, *Chinese Painting: Leading Masters and Principles*, 7 vols. (London: Lund Humphries, 1956-58), 6:pl. 9.

70. Welch, *Taoism*, p. 147. See also James C. Y. Watt, *Chinese Jades from Han to Ch'ing* (New York: Asia Society, 1980), no. 106.

71. Published in Suzuki, *Chūgoku*, 3:no. JM1-078.

72. Saso, *Teachings*, p. 57.

73. Albert Chan, *The Glory and Fall of the Ming Dynasty* (Norman: University of Oklahoma Press, 1982), pp. 109-111.

74. Sir Harry Garner, *Oriental Blue and White*, 3d ed. (London and Boston: Faber and Faber, 1970), pp. 31-32.

Color Plates

[1] LAOZI RIDING AN OX. Album leaf, ink and colors on silk, 24.3 x 22.6 cm. Chen Hongshou (1598-1652), late Ming-early Qing dynasty. John L. Severance Fund, CMA 79.27(b)

18

[6] THE IMMORTAL ZHONGLI QUAN. Hanging scroll, ink and colors on silk, 134.5 x 57.2 cm. Attributed to Zhao Qi (late fifteenth century), Ming dynasty. Purchase from the J. H. Wade Fund, CMA 76.13

19

20

22

23

24

Catalogue

however, Laozi is characterized as the humble Zhou dynasty figure who was known to all Chinese as the first sage of Daoism.

This painting is from an album of twenty leaves, painted for a friend of the artist named Lin Zhongqing. The figure, ox, and landscape are painted in very fine, elastic lines of modulated width, with the addition of pale washes of green, red, and ochre pigments. Laozi is portrayed as a sympathetic old man, dressed in flowing robes and holding a flowering branch in one hand. He rides the ox along the bank of a shallow stream bounded by rocks. Several stalks of bamboo entwined with morning glories grow along the right border of the painting. The artist's signature, in the lower right corner, is written in his elegant standard script: "Respectfully painted by [Chen] Hongshou" (Hongshou jing tu). Next to the signature is a single square-intaglio seal: "Seal of Chen Hongshou" (Chen Hongshou yin). A seal of the recipient, Lin Zhongqing, appears in the lower left corner; it reads: "Zhongqing."

1 LAOZI RIDING AN OX
Album leaf, ink and colors on silk, 24.3 x 22.6 cm.
Chen Hongshou (1598-1652), late Ming-early Qing dynasty
John L. Severance Fund, CMA 79.27(b)

In this painting the late Ming artist Chen Hongshou presents the traditional image of Laozi (Master Lao), an image reflected in the near-contemporary Ming encyclopedia *Sancai tuhui* of 1607 (Figure 1a).[1] Laozi is portrayed riding an ox on his way to the Western Regions. Since the early Han dynasty, Laozi was seen as the undisputed author of the great Daoist classic, *The Way and Its Power (Daode Jing).* According to one tradition, Laozi was an archivist at the imperial Zhou dynasty court in the early sixth century BC.[2] When he reached the venerable age of one hundred sixty, he decided to leave China and travel to the West. On the way, he was stopped by the gate-keeper Yin Xi at the Han'gu Pass (see Introduction, Figure I). Yin asked Laozi to transmit his knowledge of the Dao, and the result was the classic of some five thousand characters known as the *Daode Jing.* Since the Han dynasty, this book has been the fundamental text of the Daoist philosophy and religion. The earliest known edition of the *Daode Jing* was ex-

cavated in 1973 from the Han Tomb No. 3 of 168 BC at Mawangdui near Changsha, Hunan Province.[3]

Underlying the image of Laozi in later Chinese history was the belief that he was a manifestation of the deity known as Taishang Laojun (the Supreme Ultimate Lord Lao). The semi-historical sage Laozi had been deified in the late second century AD, during the reign of the Han Emperor Huandi.[4] During the Six Dynasties Period (third-sixth centuries AD), a complex theory regarding Laozi appeared, claiming that he had existed as a deity before the division of Yin, Yang, and all phenomenal reality out of the primordial Chaos. At different times in human history, according to this hagiography, Laozi manifested himself among men.[5] One of the key reasons behind this retroactive deification was the widespread popularity (and perceived threat) of Buddhism in the late Han and Six Dynasties periods. By claiming that Laozi had existed as a god long before the historical Buddha was born, Daoists could argue that Buddhism was merely an offshoot of a much older Chinese religion. An important aspect of this argument was the Conversion of the Barbarians theory, or Huahu, which claimed that after Laozi left China, he went to India and converted the Buddha to Daoism.[6] In Chen Hongshou's painting,

Figure 1a. *Laozi Riding an Ox* (after *Sancai tuhui*, 1607).

PUBLISHED: Osvald Sirén, *Chinese Painting: Leading Masters and Principles*, 7 vols. (London: Lund Humphries, 1956-58), 7: 164.

Eight Dynasties of Chinese Painting: The Collections of the Nelson Gallery-Atkins Museum, Kansas City, and The Cleveland Museum of Art (Cleveland, 1980), no. 209 (hereafter cited as *Eight Dynasties*).

NOTES:

1. *Sancai tuhui* (1607), chap. 10:16a-17b.

2. Arthur Waley, *The Way and Its Power: A Study of the Tao Te Ching and Its Place in Chinese Thought* (New York: Grove Press, 1958), pp. 106-108; Holmes Welch, *Taoism: The Parting of the Way* (Boston: Beacon Press, 1957), pp. 1-3.

3. Gao Heng and Chi Xizhao, "Shitan Mawangdui Han mu zhong di boshu Laozi," *Wenwu*, no. 11, 1974, 1-7; Jan Yun-hua, "The Silk Manuscripts on Taoism," *T'oung Pao*, 63, no. 1 (1977), 65-78. See also Jin Yong, "Books Copied on Silk from Han Tomb No. 3 at Mawangdui," in *New Archaeological Finds in China, II* (Beijing: Foreign Languages Press, 1978), 65-69.

4. Arthur Pontynen, "The Deification of Laozi in Chinese History and Art," *Oriental Art*, 26, no. 2 (Summer 1980), 192-200, and "The Dual Nature of Laozi in Chinese History and Art," idem, no. 3 (Autumn 1980), 308-313.

5. Laozi's various earthly manifestations in antiquity are illustrated in a handscroll entitled, *The Transformations of Laojun*, attributed to the Song dynasty painter Wang Liyong, in the Nelson-Atkins Museum, Kansas City; published in *Eight Dynasties*, no. 18.

6. On the Huahu theory, see Pontynen, "Deification," p. 193.

2 THE CELESTIAL MASTER ZHANG DAOLING

Handscroll, ink on paper, 26 x 73.9 cm.
Liang Kai (active early thirteenth century), Southern Song dynasty
Mr. and Mrs. Wan-go H. C. Weng Collection, Lyme, New Hampshire

Painted in the refined "plain-outline" or "uncolored line drawing" (baimaio) technique in ink on paper, this handscroll depicts Zhang Daoling, the first Celestial Master of the late Han dynasty (second century AD). Zhang Daoling was born in Jiangsu Province, but later moved to Sichuan Province in southwest China.[1]

After being visited in AD 142 in Sichuan by the deified spirit of Laozi (Taishang Laojun), Zhang Daoling established himself as a Daoist teacher, focusing his energies on the cultivation of longevity, healing, meditation, and the study of sacred texts such as the *Daode Jing*.

Zhang Daoling's following grew until it comprised an independent theocratic state, the members of which paid an annual tribute of five bushels of rice to their leader. Thus Zhang's movement acquired the alternate name "Five Bushels of Rice" sect. Zhang Daoling's spiritual power derived from his command of the *Twenty-Four Auspicious Alliance Registers*, consisting of lists of spirits and their attributes.[2] The devout practitioner, if properly purified, could call on these spirits for divine assistance. According to later accounts in the Daoist canon (*Daocang*), Zhang Daoling developed an elixir of immortality, of which he drank only half in order to remain on earth to assist his followers in reaching perfection.[3] There is no direct evidence, however, that Zhang Daoling was an alchemist.[4] His sect came to be known as the Way of the Celestial Masters (Tian shi dao), and the later patriarchs of the Orthodox Unity sect (Zhengyi) of southern China traced their lineage to him.

The Celestial Master appears at the center of Liang Kai's painting, seated on a lotus throne and surrounded by male and female immortal attendants and guardians. From this setting it is clear that by the Song dynasty Zhang Daoling was himself seen as a deified immortal. In the foreground a supplicant kneels before the Celestial Master. This figure's official tablet (hu), which he holds in his hands, indicates that he has just attained immortality and is presenting himself as a new official in the celestial bureaucracy. Around the central group of figures are billowing clouds and beams of light, indications that the scene takes place in heaven.

Smaller scenes, on either side of this central group, illustrate aspects of Daoist life as expressed in the teachings of Zhang Daoling. These scenes are divided into spatial cells by beautifully painted landscape and architectural elements. At the opening of the scroll on the right are three scenes illustrating life in a Daoist monastery. At the top are figures of monks painting images and worshipping a statue of the Celestial Master. The next scene depicts Daoist monks taking their meals, while the lower scene shows a group of Daoist priests being visited by their celestial counterparts, who descend to earth among swirling clouds.

The three scenes at the end of the scroll are also vertically arranged. The topmost depicts Daoists giving alms to beggars, while the next scene shows people releasing birds from cages. The lowest scene portrays a devout soul being released from the torments of hell and being greeted by the Celestial Master as he ascends to paradise. The format of the scroll, with the Celestial Master and attendants at the center and ancillary scenes on a smaller scale to the sides, is borrowed directly from Song and earlier painted frontispieces to Buddhist sūtras, or holy texts.

In the lower left corner of the scroll is the artist's minute signature: "Your servant, Liang Kai" (Chen Liang Kai). The presence of the character chen indicates that the painting was done during Liang Kai's tenure as a painter-in-attendance (daizhao) at the Southern Song court in Lin'an (Hangzhou) in the Jiatai reign period (1201-1204) of Emperor Ningzong.[5] This is most likely an early work, for after his employ at court Liang Kai spent the remainder of his life as a painter in a Chan (Zen) Buddhist temple near the capital. Although the orthodox Daoist subject matter of this scroll is unusual in the light of the predominant Chan Buddhist themes in his surviving oeuvre, other Daoist paintings by Liang Kai are

recorded in early literature.[6] The theme of the Daoist Celestial Master is also consistent with the patronage of orthodox Daoism by the Song emperors, which reached its peak under Emperor Huizong (r. 1101-1126). The tradition of pictorial depictions of Zhang Daoling began as early as Gu Kaizhi (ca. 344-ca. 406) in the Six Dynasties Period.[7]

Liang Kai's painting is followed by a transcription of the Classic of the Yellow Court (Huangting Jing) in standard script, or kaishu, attributed to the eminent Yuan dynasty artist and calligrapher Zhao Mengfu (1254-1322).[8] Following this text is a colophon by the Ming dynasty critic Wang Zhideng (1535-1612) and a note of authentication by the early Qing collector Da Zhongguang (1623-1692). Wang Zhideng's colophon reads:

Zhao Ronglu's [Zhao Mengfu's] copy of the Huangting Jing, with a painting by Liang Kai. [Liang] Kai often used burnt ink [jiao mo] in his paintings, following his inspiration with dots and washes. Everyone places his works in the untrammelled category [yi pin]. Only in this painting was his brushwork refined and detailed, and the subtle and secret mysteries entered his brush-tip. From this one knows there was nothing the ancients were unable to master.

Master Zhao's calligraphy also conveys the utmost strength, and in his copy there is not a single line that does not resemble [the original]. Now the "Goose Classic" [the Huangting Jing] is considered the finest work by the General of the Right [Wang Xizhi, 309-365], and this work should certainly be called the finest work by Ronglu [Zhao Mengfu].

In past years I heard that this scroll belonged to the family of Qi Wan of Yan Shan [in Hebei Province]. It was said that it then passed from the official's collection and entered the Jiangnan area, and was obtained by the Gu family of Shanghai. I do not know by what fate it again passed among men. One thus knows that like the brilliance of the sun and moon, [knowledge of its existence] spread like wildfire. The Zhaoling manuscript [Wang Xizhi's "Orchid Pavilion Preface"], and the Jade Fish and Golden Bowl, all emerged like this handscroll.[9] Now it has been traded, [and yet] like ripping open a fish's belly [to reveal a treasure], how could it be secretly stored away?

The handscroll is recorded in the late Ming critic Zhang Chou's Qinghe shuha fang (preface dated 1616; chap. 9:49b).

PUBLISHED: James Cahill, The Art of Southern Sung China (New York: Asia Society, 1962), no. 30.

Sherman E. Lee, "Liang K'ai," in Encyclopedia of World Art (New York: McGraw-Hill, 1963), pl. 129.

Bradley Smith and Wan-go Weng, China: A History in Art (New York: Harry Abrams, 1972), 184-185.

Sherman E. Lee, "Listening to the Ch'in by Liu Sung-nien," The Bulletin of The Cleveland Museum of Art, 73 (November 1986), fig. 8.

Xie Zhiliu, "Lun Liang Kai 'Huangting Jing shen xiang tu zhuan,'" Yiyuan duoying, 43 (1987), 1, 5-9.

NOTES:

1. On Zhang Daoling, see Michael Saso, The Teachings of Taoist Master Chuang (New Haven and London: Yale University Press, 1978), pp. 26-28.

2. Ibid., pp. 34-35.

3. Ibid., p. 27. Saso has pointed out the similarity of this account to the role of the Bodhisattva in Mahayana Buddhist philosophy.

4. Michel Strickmann, "On the Alchemy of T'ao Hung-ching," in Holmes Welch and Anna Seidel, eds., Facets of Taoism (New Haven and London: Yale University Press,1979), p. 167.

5. Xia Wenyan, Tuhui baojian (1365; Huashi congshu ed.), chap. 4:104, 776.

6. See, for example, Liang's paintings of Zhong Kui (the Daoist demon queller) listed in Bian Yongyu, Shigutang shuhua huikao (1682), chap. 2:138, and Zhuangzi Dreaming of a Butterfly, recorded in Chen Jîru, Nigulu (ca. 1635), chap. 4:9.

7. Yu Jianhua, Zhongguo hualun leibian, 2 vols. (1956; reprint Hong Kong: Zhonghua shuju, 1973), 1:581-582, translated in William Acker, Some T'ang and Pre-T'ang Texts on Chinese Painting, 2 vols. (Leiden: E. J. Brill, 1954), vol. 1, pt. 2, pp. 73-82.

8. On the Huangting Jing, see [3].

9. Wang Zhideng refers to the burial of Wang Xizhi's most famous work, the Orchid Pavilion Preface (Lanting xu) in the tomb of the Tang emperor Taizong (r. 626-649). In fact, Wang Xizhi's original was never seen again, and Wang Zhideng undoubtedly referred to the numerous copies of the Tang period, some of which may have been confused for the original; see Lothar Ledderose, Mi Fu and the Classical Tradition of Chinese Calligraphy (Princeton: Princeton University Press, 1979), p. 20.

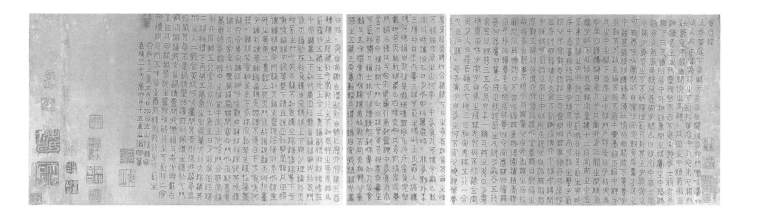

3 CLASSIC OF THE YELLOW COURT
(HUANGTING JING)
Handscroll, ink on paper, 23.2 x
78.7 cm.
Wen Zhengming (1470-1559), Ming
dynasty
Ssu Isabel and I-hsüeh Hugo Weng Collection

In this scroll the great Ming dynasty scholar, painter, and calligrapher Wen Zhengming transcribed the text of one the earliest Daoist classics of the Mao Shan, or Shangqing (Great Clarity) sect, the *Classic of the Yellow Court (Huangting Jing)*. Specifically, Wen Zhengming transcribed the earlier, "outer" version of the classic (*Huangting waijing jing*).[1] According to tradition, this book was revealed to the female Daoist adept Wei Huacun (251-334) by perfected beings from the heaven of Great Clarity.[2]

The *Huangting Jing* is a text on meditation, written in the arcane language of alchemy. It guides the practitioner through the vital centers of the human body, the purpose of which is "gradually to refine the spirits within the [human] microcosm until finally the state of void or primordial simplicity [hundun] is reached."[3] This is equivalent to union with the Dao.

The most famous version of the *Huangting jing* was written in standard script (kaishu) by the Sage of Calligraphy, Wang Xizhi (309-365) in AD 356.[4] This transcription, one of the greatest works of standard script in the history of Chinese calligraphy, was believed to have been in the imperial collection during the early Tang dynasty, but was destroyed during the An Lushan rebellion of 755-756.[5] Nevertheless, the form and style of the original were transmitted to later generations through the medium of ink rubbings. There is no question that Wen Zhengming—one of the finest connoisseurs of calligraphy of the Ming dynasty—would have known Wang Xizhi's transcription.

Despite the near-divine status enjoyed by the Wang Xizhi model, Wen decided to transcribe the *Huangting Jing* in the ancient seal script of the Bronze Age. As has been shown in a recent discussion of this work, Wen's use of seal script gives the work an even more archaic flavor than would have attached to the use of standard script.[6] Considering Wen Zhengming's distance in time from the original, it is not surprising that he chose an archaic script for an ancient and difficult Daoist text. Furthermore, the primitive yet elegant seal script comes closest of all calligraphic forms to the mysterious shapes of Daoist talismans, and the aesthetic resonance between the two is directly conveyed in Wen Zhengming's transcription, executed at the age of eighty-eight.[7]

According to the late Ming critic Wang Shizhen's *Yiyuan zhiyan* of 1577, Wen Zhengming based his seal script on the writing of the Tang dynasty seal-script master Li Yangbing (late eighth century).[8] Comparable examples of Wen Zhengming's seal-script calligraphy can be seen in his transcriptions of the *Thousand Character Classic*, dated 1536 and 1548, in the National Palace Museum, Taipei.[9]

PUBLISHED: Tseng Yu-ho Ecke, *Chinese Calligraphy* (Philadelphia: Philadelphia Museum of Art, 1971), no. 50.
Richard Edwards, ed., *The Art of Wen Cheng-ming* (Ann Arbor: University of Michigan Museum of Art, 1976), no. 60.

NOTES:
1. On the difference between the two versions (the other being the slightly later *Huangting neijing jing*, or "inner" version), see Lothar Ledderose, *Mi Fu and the Classical Tradition of Chinese Calligraphy* (Princeton: Princeton University Press, 1979), p. 70.

2. Michael Saso, *The Teachings of Taoist Master Chuang* (New Haven and London, 1978), p. 37.

3. Ibid., p. 279, n.112.

4. Published in *Shodō zenshu*, 25 vols. (Tokyo: Heibonsha, 1960), 4:pls. 8-9.

5. Ledderose, *Mi Fu*, pp. 70-71.

6. Edwards, ed., *Wen Cheng-ming*, no. 60, p. 204.

7. Cf. Lazlo Legeza, *Tao Magic: The Chinese Art of the Occult* (London: Thames and Hudson, 1975), pl. 69.

8. Quoted in Ma Zonghuo, *Shulin zaojian* (1934; reprint, Beijing: Wenwu chubanshe, 1984), chap. 11:311. On Li Yangbing see Shen Fu, et al., *Traces of the Brush: Studies in Chinese Calligraphy* (New Haven: Yale University Press, 1977), p. 44.

9. Published in National Palace Museum, *Wupai jiushi nian zhan* (Taipei: National Palace Museum, 1975), nos. 137, 163.

4 XU XUN MOVING HIS FAMILY TO PARADISE
Hanging scroll, ink and colors on silk,
165.6 x 64.1 cm.
Cui Zizhong (d. 1644), late Ming dynasty
Mr. and Mrs. William H. Marlatt Fund,
CMA 61.90

This painting by Cui Zizhong depicts the early Six Dynasties Period Daoist Xu Xun (240-374) moving his family to paradise. Xu was born in Nanchang, Jiangxi Province, and studied Daoism with the famous magician Wu Meng. He then served as a model Confucian official in Jingyang, Sichuan Province, and is thus often referred to as Xu Jingyang. Xu became famous as a wise administrator and occasionally helped the local people through feats of magic. He was traditionally seen as the founder of the Thunder Magic sects of Daoism, and specifically of the Qingming zhongxiao sect.[1] He taught his entire family Daoist meditation, and when he attained the age of one hundred thirty-four in AD 374, he took his family and ascended to paradise. He was first venerated as an immortal at the imperial Song dynasty court under Emperor Huizong in 1112.

In the center of the painting, Xu appears with his family, riding like Laozi on an ox. He is dressed in a red robe and wears the square cap of a Daoist. One of his wives rides in a cart pulled by a servant, while a second wife rides on an ox, holding a small child. Two female servants walk alongside the cart, one carrying an infant. Below, three other figures trail behind. They bring double-gourds (symbols of the joining of earth and heaven), a lute (qin) in its silk bag, a chicken in a basket, and a dog on a leash. The chicken and dog allude to a passage in the *Daode Jing*, describing the ancient utopian society in which men lived in such harmonious proximity that the crowing chickens and barking dogs of adjacent villages were easily audible. In all, there are fifteen figures in the painting.

The landscape is outlined in monochrome ink, with red, blue, green, and pale orange colors added to the figures and foliage. The rocks are sharply outlined and minimally shaded. Occasionally pale, scumbled texture strokes are laid over the washes. The unnatural lighting of these rock surfaces, the jagged outlines of the tree trunks, and the lapidary patterning of the flora suggest that Xu Xun and his family have already entered a Daoist paradise.

Two seals of Cui Zizhong appear in the lower left corner, reading: "North sea" (Bei hai) and "Seal of Cui Zizhong" (Cui

chaic styles of Gu Kaizhi (ca. 344-406), Lu Tanwei (fifth century), Yan Liben (seventh century), and Wu Daozi (eighth century), Cui Zizhong created a highly stylized vision of antiquity. He was reportedly admired by Dong Qichang (1555-1636), one of the great arbiters of taste in the late Ming, whom he met in 1633.[3] Cui Zizhong died as a pauper in 1644, the year of the fall of the Ming dynasty.

There is a similar painting of Xu Xun by Cui Zizhong in the National Palace Museum, Taipei, in which only five figures appear.[4] It is inscribed with a poem and note by Cui, reading as follows:

He moved his household to escape vulgarity and study the refining of cinnabar,
Leading his wife and children, together they entered the mountains.
From this we know that there are chickens and dogs in the clouds,
There they live and grow—no different than among men.

Every master [of painting] *has a model for* The Zhenren Xu with Chickens and Dogs among the Clouds. *I have gone back and taken antiquity as my master, and have not been soiled by them* [the lifeless copies]. *I painted this for master Nanpu; recorded by Cui Zizhong of Chang'an* [Beijing].

Zizhong yin). There are also collectors' seals of Xiang Yuan and Tang Zuomei (both late eighteenth-early nineteenth century), Zhang Heng (1915-1963), and Wang Jiqian (b. 1909). Cui Zizhong, the artist, was an early seventeenth-century painter who worked for most of his life in the Ming dynasty capital, Beijing.[2] Although a respected scholar, he progressed no further than the xiucai (baccalaureate) degree. He therefore gave up the pursuit of an official career, becoming a professional painter. Famous for both his figures and landscapes, he was renowned for his eccentricity. Inspired by the ar-

PUBLISHED: *Eight Dynasties of Chinese Painting*, no. 209.

NOTES:

1. See Michael Saso, *The Teachings of Taoist Master Chuang* (New Haven and London: Yale University Press, 1978), p. 53; also Akizuki Kan'ei, "Kyo Son Kyodai to Jomei-chuko-do ni tsuite," *Dōkyo kenkyu*, 3 (1966), 197-235.

2. For biographical information on Cui Zizhong, see James Cahill, *The Distant Mountains: Chinese Painting of the Late Ming Dynasty, 1570-1644* (New York and Tokyo: Weatherhill, 1982), pp. 224-226, 243-244; and *Style Transformed: A Special Exhibition of Five Late Ming Artists* (Taipei: National Palace Museum, 1977), pp. 36-39.

3. Cahill, *Distant Mountains*, p. 255.

4. *Style Transformed*, no. 72. Another version of the same theme by Cui, unpublished, is in the Palace Museum, Beijing.

5 MOUNTAINS OF THE IMMORTALS
Handscroll, ink and colors on silk, 33 x 102.9 cm.
Chen Ruyan (ca. 1331-1371), Yuan dynasty
Mrs. A. Dean Perry Collection

Chen Ruyan's handscroll depicts a Daoist paradise, the forms of which are alive with a flame-like energy. The painting begins at the upper right with a distant mountain, visible beyond a hazy valley. Then a mountain range appears, the peaks of which rise to precipitous heights.

A temple is situated in a narrow valley that becomes increasingly steep as it ascends. In a clearing below, an immortal rests on a carpet next to a qin, ritual vessels, and several lingzhi mushrooms (see [25]). He watches his servant, who teaches two cranes to dance. Behind and above these figures, swirling clouds drift down from the peaks. These clouds are the manifestation of the earth's inner breath (qi), which nourishes the trees and magic fungi of the landscape.

As the scroll progresses to the left, a range of cliffs rises up to the top of the painting. Steep clefts appear in the rocks; from two of them flow waterfalls, out of

another walks an immortal. High above, another immortal glides through the air on a crane. The painting ends with a clearing enclosed by peaks. In this geomantically protected space, immortals walk among the trees, rocks, and auspicious fauna.

Chen Ruyan's painting illustrates the concept of an immortals' paradise as envisaged by Daoists from the Six Dynasties Period onward. The use of azurite and malachite pigments in the landscape suggests an antique mood through its association with Tang dynasty and earlier painting styles. In addition, these minerals, along with cinnabar, were key ingredients

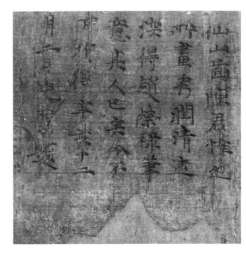

in certain elixirs of immortality. Their appearance in Daoist paintings thus alluded to the realm of the immortals.[1] The entire painting was first outlined in ink alone, and then heavy green and blue pigments were added to the landscape. The trees have deep brown trunks, and yellow and red pigments are used in the figures and foliage.

Chen Ruyan (ca. 1331-1371) lived for most of his life in Suzhou, Jiangsu Province.[2] He was a close friend of the famous painters Ni Zan (1301-1374) and Wang Meng (1308-1385), as well as the wealthy collector Gu Ying (1310-1369). When the enlightened rebel leader Zhang Shicheng took control of Suzhou from the Mongols toward the end of the Yuan dynasty, Chen served as a military advisor to Pan Yuanming, Zhang's brother-in-law.[3] After the establishment of the Ming dynasty in 1368, Chen Ruyan traveled to the new capital at Nanjing, and was then appointed registrar (jingli) of Jinan, Shandong Province.[4] Due to an unknown offense, Chen was executed in the autumn of 1371.

Although the painting is unsigned, it bears an inscription by Ni Zan in the upper right corner that identifies Chen Ruyan as the artist (see detail of [5]). This is written in a spare, fluid standard script (kaishu), derived from the archaic style of the Three Kingdoms Period calligrapher Zhong You (third century AD).[5] In his inscription, Ni Zan alludes to Chen's death, stating that Chen's paintings could no longer be obtained:

Mountains of the Immortals *was painted by Master Chen Weiyun* [Chen Ruyan]. *In its rich elegance and pure detachment, he has profoundly captured the brush-spirit of Zhao Ronglu* [Zhao Mengfu, 1254-1322]. *Who else could have done this? Now one can no longer obtain* [his works]. *On the second day of the twelfth month of the year xinhai* [1371], *inscribed by Ni Zan.*

Ni's inscription was written only several months after Chen Ruyan's death. His mention of the early Yuan master Zhao Mengfu as the stylistic model for Chen's handscroll is corroborated by several of Zhao's surviving blue-and-green style landscapes.[6]
Mountains of the Immortals was Chen Ruyan's best-known work from the fifteenth century onward.[7] It bears the seals of many famous collectors, including Xiang Yuanbian (1525-1590), Zhu Zhichi (late Ming dynasty), Liang Qingbiao (1620-1691), Gao Shiqi (1645-1704), and Lu Xinyuan (1834-1894).[8]

PUBLISHED: Sherman E. Lee and Wai-kam Ho, *Chinese Art under the Mongols: The Yüan Dynasty, 1279-1368* (Cleveland: The Cleveland Museum of Art, 1968), no. 264.
Eight Dynasties of Chinese Painting, no. 114.
Richard M. Barnhart, *Along the Border of Heaven* (New York: Metropolitan Museum of Art, 1983), p. 116, figs. 51, 52.
Susan E. Nelson, "Intimations of Immortality in Chinese Landscape Painting of the Fourteenth Century," *Oriental Art*, 33, no. 3 (Autumn 1987), fig. 1.

NOTES:
1. See John Hay, *Kernels of Energy, Bones of Earth: The Rock in Chinese Art* (New York: China Institute, 1985), pp. 46-50.

2. Xu Qin, *Ming hua lu* (1673; *Huashi congshu* ed.), chap. 2:19.

3. Lee and Ho, *Chinese Art under the Mongols*, no. 264.

4. L. Carrington Goodrich and Fang Chao-ying, *Dictionary of Ming Biography*, 2 vols. (New York: Columbia University Press, 1976), 1:163-165.

5. On the sources of Ni Zan's calligraphy, see Ma Zonghuo, *Shulin zaojian* (1934; reprint Beijing: Wenwu chubanshe, 1984), chap. 10:278, and Wen Fong, et al., *Images of the Mind* (Princeton: Princeton University Art Museum, 1984), p. 113.

6. See, for example, Zhao's *Mind-Landscape of Xie Youyu* in the John B. Elliott Collection on loan to the Princeton University Art Museum, published in Wen Fong, et al., *Images of the Mind* (Princeton: University Art Gallery, 1984), no. 6. See also Richard Vinograd, "Some Landscapes Related to the Blue-and-Green Manner from the Early Yüan Period," *Artibus Asiae*, 41, nos. 2-3 (1979), 130, figs. 11, 18, and Barnhart, *Along the Border of Heaven*, p. 116.

7. It is first recorded as a famous work in Du Mu's *Yuyi bian* (ca. 1500; *Meishu congshu* ed.), pp. 287-288.

8. For a complete record of the scroll's documentation, see *Eight Dynasties*, no. 114. Gao Shiqi also owned other objects in the present exhibition: the Yan Hui handscroll depicting the Daoist demon queller Zhong Kui [7], and the silver raft-cup of 1345 by Zhu Bishan [19].

6 THE IMMORTAL ZHONGLI QUAN

Hanging scroll, ink and colors on silk, 134.5 x 57.2 cm.
Attributed to Zhao Qi (late fifteenth century), Ming dynasty
Purchase from the J. H. Wade Fund, CMA 76.13

Zhongli Quan was said to have been born during the Han dynasty, although one Song dynasty source states that "his dates are unknown."[1] Aside from being the chief among the Eight Immortals, he was also well-known as the teacher of the immortal Lü Dongbin (Figure X). His biography in the Ming compendium *The Complete Biographies of Immortals (Liexian quanzhuan)* of 1598 states that he was born in a time of realized men (zhen ren) in high antiquity and that his father was a palace official. The miraculous events of his life that led to his attainment of immortality are related as follows:

At his birth a strange light shone around him, appearing like bright flames, and the imperial bodyguards were all alarmed. He had a round head, a broad forehead, large ears, long eyebrows, deep-set eyes, a lofty nose, a square mouth,[2] a large jaw, and a complexion like cinnabar.

When he was a boy of three sui [two years], *he once made no sound, and neither laughed nor ate for several days. After seven days had passed, he jumped up suddenly and said, "I have traveled to the Purple Mansions* [i.e., the realm of the immortals], *and my name is written in the Jade Capital."*

He was very strong. During the Han dynasty he served as a great general. Once, when attacking Turfan [in Central Asia], *his side lost the advantage. He alone escaped on horse-back and rode into a mountain valley. He lost the road, and at night entered a dense forest. There he came upon a barbarian monk, with disheveled hair brushing his forehead. On the monk's body hung a robe of knotted grass. The monk led him for several li[3] until they saw a village, and said, "This is where Master Donghua attained the Dao. Here you can rest." He then bowed and disappeared.*

Zhongli was not inclined to rush into the village. After some time, he heard someone say, "This must be the one the blue-eyed barbarian spoke of." He saw an old man wearing a white deerskin and holding a green bramble staff. The old man raised his voice and said, "Is this not the great general Zhongli Quan? Why didn't you spend the night where the monk lives?" Zhongli heard him and was much alarmed, for he knew this was no ordinary person.

At that point the place was transformed into a rude lair, and he found himself thinking of Luan birds and cranes [the attributes of immortals]. He then turned his mind to the Dao, and begged the old man for the method of transcending the world. Thereupon the old man transmitted to him the Secrets of Extended Life (chang sheng), the Fiery Transformations of Gold and Cinnabar, and the Green Dragon Sword Technique. Zhongli then took his leave and emerged from his gate. When he turned around and looked back toward the village, there was nothing to see.

Later on he encountered the zhen ren Huayang, who transmitted to him the Interior Elixir of the Spatula and the Fire Talismans of Tai Yi [the Supreme Ultimate]. He also met the immortal Wang Xuanfu, from whom he obtained the secrets of longevity. Traveling through the clouds, he arrived in Lu [in Shandong Province] and lived in Zoucheng. Once he entered the Kongtong [Mountains], and dwelt at the Peak of the Four Graybeards of Purple-Cinnabar. Again he obtained the Secrets of the Jade Casket, whereupon he became an immortal and left the world.[4]

It is likely that this painting was originally one of a set depicting the Eight Immortals. Zhongli Quan is shown crossing the ocean waves and holding a double-gourd in his hand. He has intense, bulging eyes, a fine beard, and a bare stomach. He is dressed in flowing robes, painted with bold lines of varying width. Around his waist is a belt of leaves, a common part of immortals' garb. Pale green, white, red, and brown pigments are added within the ink outlines. Painted in fluctuating lines, the coiling waves send forth white beads of spray as they break. As Sherman Lee has shown, the scroll has been cut down slightly from its original size in previous remountings.[5]

Although unsigned, the painting can be confidently attributed to the late fifteenth-century Zhe School painter Zhao Qi.[6] Zhao's name is unrecorded as a painter in traditional Chinese sources, but he was most likely a contemporary of Liu Jun, who worked as a court painter in the Forbidden City during the reign of the Hongzhi Emperor (r. 1488-1505). The attribution to Zhao Qi is supported by a similar depiction of the immortal Liu Haichan in the Nezu Museum, Tokyo (Figure 6a), which is signed "Zhao Qi" and which bears the seal: "Daily approaching the pure and radiant [the emperor]" (Ri jin qingguang). The same seal was also used by the Hongzhi court painters Lü Ji and Lü Wenying.[7] Zhao Qi's style, while close to that of Liu Jun, can be distinguished by the more jagged lineament in the drapery. In contrast, Liu's drapery patterns are generally more fluid. The styles of the two painters, however, are often very similar, and it is likely that they worked in the same palace workshop and shared the same assistants.

PUBLISHED: *Eight Dynasties of Chinese Painting*, no. 132.

NOTES:
1. *Xuanhe shupu* (1120; *Yishu congbian* ed.), chap. 19:441-442. The Song Emperor Huizong owned an example of what was believed to be an original cursive script handscroll by Zhongli Quan, the forms of which were "derived from dragons and snakes."

2. The statement that Zhongli had a mouth that was "square" (kou fang) had the added meaning of "honest [i.e., morally square] mouth," or "his words were honest."

3. A *li* is approximately one-third of a mile.

4. Wang Shizhen, comp., *Liexian quanzhuan* (1598), chap. 3:6a-b; reprinted in *Zhongguo gudai banhua congkan* (Shanghai, 1961). This account presents the traditional view of Zhongli Quan as accepted in the Ming dynasty. Such accounts may in fact reflect the blending in the popular imagination of composite personalities. The task of sifting through earlier literary sources and charting the evolving hagiographies of the Eight Immortals (and other immortals) has yet to be accomplished.

5. *Eight Dynasties*, no. 132.

6. Ibid.

7. James Cahill, *Parting at the Shore: Chinese Painting of the Early and Middle Ming Dynasty, 1368-1580* (New York and Tokyo: Weatherhill, 1978), p. 108.

33

Figure 6a. *Liu Haichan.* Hanging scroll, ink and colors on silk. Zhao Qi, late fifteenth century, Ming dynasty. Nezu Museum, Tokyo.

7 ZHONG KUI ON A NIGHT EXCURSION WITH DEMONS
Handscroll, ink on silk, 24.8 x 240.3 cm.
Yan Hui (active late thirteenth-early fourteenth century), Yuan dynasty
Mr. and Mrs. William H. Marlatt Fund, CMA 61.206

This handscroll features the Daoist demon queller, Zhong Kui, on a nocturnal outing with a procession of demons. The story of Zhong Kui dates from the Tang dynasty and is recorded in Chen Wenzhu's *Tianzhong ji (1589)*:

One afternoon in the Kaiyuan era [713-742], *Minghuang* [the emperor Xuanzong], *feeling ill after he had returned from a round of bow-and-arrow practice on Li Shan, fell asleep. He soon saw in a dream a small demon, wearing only knee-length trousers and one shoe—the other being tied at his waist—and holding a bamboo fan, in the act of stealing the favorite consort's embroidered perfume-bag and his own jade flute. Then, instead of escaping, the strange being began frolicking around the palace grounds with the loot. Minghuang therefore approached him and demanded an explanation. The demon respectfully replied that his name was Xu Hao and explained that "Xu" stood for "stealing indiscriminately for the sake of*

fun" and "Hao" for "replacing man's joys with sorrows." Hearing this, the emperor became angry and wanted to call for his bodyguards. But at that very moment, a large demon, wearing a tattered hat, blue robe, horn waist-belt, and black boots appeared and nabbed the thief. Immediately afterwards, he proceeded first to gouge out the victim's eyes, then tore him to pieces and finally ate him.

When the emperor asked him who he was, the Demon Queller introduced himself as Zhong Kui, a jinshi [candidate] *from Zhongnan, who ashamed at having failed the next higher degree of examination during the Wude era* [618-627], *had committed suicide by dashing his head against the palace steps. He further mentioned that because the emperor Gaozu awarded him an honorable burial of a court official of the green-robe rank, he had vowed to rid the world of mischievous demons like Xu Hao. At these words, Minghuang awoke and found himself fully recovered. Without delay he summoned* [the court painter] *Wu Daozi, and requested a portrait of the Demon Queller as he had seen him in his dream. When it was finished, the emperor examined it carefully and said, "You and I must have had a similar vision!" And he awarded Wu one hundred taels of gold.[1]*

The painting shows the Demon Queller and nineteen obsequious demons, three of whom carry Zhong Kui on their shoulders. Wearing the robes and hat of a Tang scholar-official, Zhong Kui glowers at the demons in front of him. The latter carry his traveling implements, including a gong, wine vessels, weapons, a folding chair, a qin, a brush, scrolls, and an inkstone. At the end of the scroll are four demons, three of whom play musical instruments while the fourth carries an umbrella over Zhong Kui's head. The figures are painted in dark, fluctuating outlines and subtly modulated ink washes; the result is an astonishing visualization of creatures from the nether world. Yan Hui's signature appears along the left border: "Yan Qiuyue." As Wai-kam Ho has shown, the painting was once followed by colophons by Yu He (dated 1389) and Wu Kuan (1435-1504), which are now attached to a copy.[2]

By the Song dynasty (960-1279), it was common for artists to paint Zhong Kui's image at the lunar New Year.[3] A painting of the Demon Queller functioned as an auspicious image and helped clear one's household of demons and other malign influences for the coming year. During the Yuan dynasty, when China was occupied by the Mongols, paintings of Zhong Kui also symbolized the desire of native

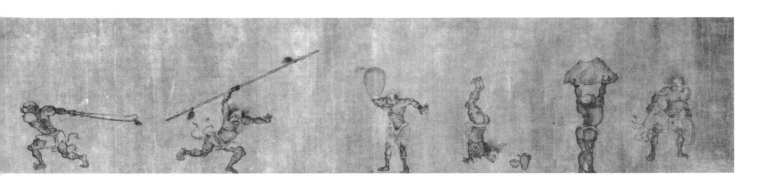

Chinese to rid their country of the Mongols, represented by the demons Zhong Kui subjugated.[4]

Yan Hui was one of the most famous painters of Daoist figures in the early Yuan dynasty. He created both wall paintings in Daoist temples and paintings on silk, several of which survive. Aside from the Cleveland handscroll, his best-known works in this genre are the pair of hanging scrolls depicting the immortals Liu Haichan and Li Tieguai in the Chion-in, Kyoto, and a single hanging scroll depicting Li Tieguai in the Palace Museum, Beijing.[5]

Yan Hui's handscroll has a title frontis-piece by the Qing dynasty scholar Niu Shuyu (1760-1827), reading: "[Yan] Qiuyue's ink-illusion" (Qiuyue mo huan). The scroll bears the collectors' seals of An Guo (1481-1534), Xiang Yuanbian (1525-1590), Geng Zhaozhong (1640-1686), Gao Shiqi (1645-1704), and Tan Jing (twentieth century).

PUBLISHED: Sherman E. Lee, "Yen Hui: The Lantern Night Excursion of Zhong Kui," *The Bulletin of The Cleveland Museum of Art*, 49 (February 1962), 36-42.
Eight Dynasties of Chinese Painting, no. 91.

NOTES:
1. Translated in Mary H. Fong, "A Probable Second 'Chung K'uei' by Emperor Shun-chih of the Ch'ing Dynasty," *Oriental Art*, 23, no. 4 (Winter 1977), 427-428.

2. *Eight Dynasties*, no. 91.

3. Howard Rogers has suggested that the traditional title of the scroll, *The Lantern-Night Excursion of Zhong Kui*, should be modified since Zhong Kui is neither associated with the lantern festival nor do lanterns appear in the painting (Cleveland, curatorial files).

4. Thomas Lawton, *Chinese Figure Painting* (Washington: Smithsonian Institution, 1973), p. 145.

5. Osvald Sirén, *Chinese Painting: Leading Masters and Principles*, 7 vols. (London: Lund Humphries, 1956-58), 6: pl. 9; Xu Bangda, *Gu shuhua jianding gailun* (Beijing: Wenwu chubanshe, 1981), pl. 46.

8 THE PEACH BLOSSOM SPRING
Hanging scroll, ink and colors on satin,
136.7 x 52.2 cm.
Liu Du (active ca. 1632-l675), late Ming-
early Qing dynasty
John L. Severance Fund, CMA 71.227

Liu Du, like Chen Hongshou [1], was a
student of the painter Lan Ying (1585-ca.
1664) and a native of Hangzhou, Zhejiang Province.[1] His hanging scroll
depicts the story of the Peach Blossom
Spring (*Taohua yuan ji),* written in the
Six Dynasties Period by Tao Qian (Tao
Yuanming, 365-427).[2] It tells the tale of
a fisherman who by chance finds a

36

secluded valley, hidden by a mysterious
cave. Living harmoniously in this Shangri-
La, removed from the vicissitudes of
strife in the outside world, were people
whose ancestors had fled the tyrannical
emperor Qin Shihuangdi of the third century BC.

As Susan Nelson has demonstrated, the
lost valley of Tao Qian's story had strong
associations with Daoist paradises; for example, the peach trees that lined the
route to the cave were associated with the
goddess Xiwangmu's peaches of immortality [17], and the cave itself alluded to
the cave-heavens (dongtian) of Daoist
lore.[3] Many later commentators on Tao's
story suggested that the inhabitants of the
Peach Blossom Spring were immortals,
particularly since the cave that led there
could never again be found.

This spirit pervades Liu Du's painting,
in which the lone fisherman rows toward
the cave opening at the center of the
painting, in which stand two immortal-like
figures. The peach trees appear here
above the cave, between the viewer and a
cluster of pavilions visible through a cleft
in the rocks. This is all that one sees of
the paradise beyond. Liu's hanging scroll
thus suggests the hidden valley instead of
openly depicting it, as is usually done in
paintings of the Peach Blossom Spring.
Features such as the stalactites in the
cave and the very inaccessibility of the
Peach Blossom Spring further enhance
the suggestion of a higher realm of immortals in the distance.

Liu Du's inscription is written in run-
ning or semi-cursive script (xingshu)
along the upper right border of the painting: "In the xiaochun [tenth] month of the
year gengyin [1650], painted after Zhao
Chengzhi [Zhao Mengfu]. Liu Du."

This is followed by two seals, reading:
"Seal of Liu Du" (Liu Du zhi yin) and
"Shuxian," the artist's courtesy name, or
zi. The date of 1650, coming six years
after the chaotic fall of the native Chinese
Ming dynasty to the foreign Manchu Qing
dynasty, is significant, for Liu's painting
may represent a conscious desire for a
more peaceful, settled time.

The painting bears two seals in the
lower right corner of the modern collector
Liu Zuochou.

PUBLISHED: *Eight Dynasties of Chinese
Painting,* no. 198.

NOTES:
1. *Eight Dynasties,* no. 198; see also
James Cahill, *The Distant Mountains:
Chinese Painting of the Late Ming Dynasty* (New York and Tokyo: Weatherhill,
1982), p. 203.

2. Translated in Burton Watson, *The Columbia Book of Chinese Poetry—From Early Times to the Thirteenth Century* (New
York: Columbia University Press, 1984),
pp. 142-143.

3. Susan Nelson, "On Through to the Beyond: The Peach Blossom Spring as Paradise," *Archives of Asian Art,* 39 (1986),
25.

Preface to the Poem on the Peach
Blossom Spring *by Tao Qian, translated
by Burton Watson.*

*During the Taiyuan era (376-397) of the
Jin dynasty, there was a man of Wuling
who caught fish for a living. Once he was
making his way up a valley stream and
had lost track of how far he had gone
when he suddenly came upon a forest of
peach trees in bloom. For several hundred
paces on either bank of the stream there
were no other trees to be seen, but fragrant
grasses, fresh and beautiful, and falling
petals whirling all around.*

*The fisherman, astonished at such a
sight, pushed ahead, hoping to see what
lay beyond the forest. Where the forest
ended there was a spring that fed the
stream, and beyond that a hill. The hill
had a small opening in it, from which
there seemed to come a gleam of light.
Abandoning his boat, the fisherman went
through the opening. At first it was very
narrow, with barely room for a person to
pass, but after he had gone twenty or thirty paces, it suddenly opened out and he
could see clearly.*

*A plain stretched before him, broad and
flat, with houses and sheds dotting it, and
rich fields, pretty ponds, and mulberry and
bamboo around them. Paths ran north
and south, east and west across the fields,
and chickens and dogs could be heard
from farm to farm. The men and women
who passed back and forth in the midst,
sowing and tilling the fields, were all
dressed just like other people, and from
white-haired elders to youngsters with their
hair unbound, everyone seemed carefree
and happy.*

*The people, seeing the fisherman, were
greatly startled and asked where he had
come from. When he had answered all
their questions, they invited him to return
with them to their home, where they set
out wine and killed a chicken to prepare a
meal.*

*As soon as the others in the village
heard of his arrival, they all came to greet
him. They told him that some generations
in the past their people had fled from the
troubled times of the Qin dynasty (221-
209 BC) and had come with their wives
and children and fellow villagers to this
faraway place. They had never ventured
out into the world again, and hence in*

time had come to be completely cut off from other people. They asked him what dynasty was ruling at present—they had not even heard of the Han dynasty, to say nothing of the Wei and Jin dynasties that succeeded it. The fisherman replied to each of their questions to the best of his knowledge, and everyone sighed with wonder.

The other villagers invited the fisherman to visit their homes as well, each setting out wine and food for him. Thus he remained for several days before taking his leave. One of the villagers said to him, "I trust you won't tell the people on the outside about this."

After the fisherman had made his way out of the place, he found his boat and followed the route he had taken earlier, taking care to note the places that he passed. When he reached the prefectural town, he went to call on the governor and repeated what had happened. The governor immediately dispatched men to go with him to look for the place, but though he tried to locate the spots that he had taken note of earlier, in the end he became confused and could not find the way again.

Liu Ziqi of Nanyang, a gentleman-recluse of lofty ideals, heard the story and began delightedly making plans to go

there, but before he could carry them out, he fell sick and died. Since then there have been no more "seekers of the ford."[1]

NOTE:

1. An allusion to *Analects XVIII, 6,* in which Confucius sends one of his disciples to inquire about a fording place across a river. Here, of course, the phrase refers to seekers of the utopian land of the Peach Blossom Spring.

9 TOMB TILE
Stamped earthenware, L. 105.4 cm.
First-second century AD, Eastern Han dynasty
Gift of Mr. and Mrs. Ralph King, CMA 15.70

The figures with striated bodies gliding among the mountains in the upper register of this tile, designed to line the wall of an underground tomb, correspond to the "feathered immortals" of early Daoist literature. The *Zhuangzi* (third century BC), for example, describes a type of spirit that lives among distant mountains:

There is a Holy Man [shen ren] *living on faraway Gushe Mountain, with skin like ice or snow, and gentle and shy like a young girl. He doesn't eat the five grains, but sucks the wind, drinks the dew, climbs up on the clouds and mist, rides a flying dragon, and wanders beyond the four seas. By concentrating his spirit, he can protect creatures from sickness and plague and make the harvest plentiful.*[1]

The *Huainanzi* of the late second century BC similarly describes immortal spirits, some with hybrid forms, that dwell in mountains and who control the wind and rain.[2] Certain mountains were considered holy from very early times in China.

These included the Five Sacred Peaks (wu yue)—Tai Shan in Shandong, southern Heng Shan in Hunan, northern Heng Shan in Hebei, Hua Shan in Shaanxi, and Song Shan in Henan—and the more elusive isles of the immortals in the eastern sea—of which Penglai, Fanghu, and Yingzhou were the most famous (see Figure II).[3] As the great Daoist alchemist Ge Hong wrote in the early fourth century AD, "whether they are large or small, all mountains are informed by the divine powers of holy spirits, great or small in proportion to the size of the mountain."[4]

The depiction of the mountain sprites in the upper register of this tomb tile reflects the widespread desire in the Han dynasty to be reborn as such an immortal. The belief in immortals who lived in sacred and remote mountains, free of the "red dust" of the world, evolved into a powerful concept in Daoism, and such figures are often seen in later Daoist art (see, for example, [5] and [21]).

Both sides of the tile are decorated with crisply stamped motifs impressed into the clay while it was still wet. At either end of the tile are openings for joining with other tiles. The top and bottom surfaces are smooth and plain. The decoration on the front and back consists of five horizontal registers enclosed within an abstract

border. Each register contains repeated motifs stamped into the wet clay. The points at which the individual motifs meet in a given register are clearly visible. In the lowest register, the first stamped pattern at the left has been partially obliterated by the contiguous and identical pattern to the immediate right.

The upper register depicts a series of mountain peaks with birds, between which appear the immortals. The second and fourth registers are stamped with identical palmette designs in diamond-shaped cartouches. The third register consists of five panels with hunters on horseback shooting at deer with crossbows. The fifth register depicts tigers chasing horses or antelope-like animals.

PUBLISHED: Anneliese G. Bulling, "Hollow Tomb Tiles: Recent Excavations and Their Dating," *Oriental Art*, 11 (Spring 1965), fig. 14.

Laurence Sickman and Alexander Soper, *The Art and Architecture of China* (Harmondsworth: Penguin Books, 1971), pls. 37, 38.

Handbook of The Cleveland Museum of Art (Cleveland, 1978), p. 329.

NOTES:

1. Burton Watson, trans., *The Complete Works of Chuang Tzu* (New York: Columbia University Press, 1968), p. 33.

2. Michael Loewe, *Chinese Ideas of Life and Death* (London: George Allen and Unwin, 1982), pp. 20-21.

3. For a list of mountains sacred to Daoism, see James Ware, *Alchemy and Religion in the China of AD 320: The Nei P'ien of Ko Hung* (Cambridge: Massachusetts Institute of Technology Press, 1966), p. 94.

4. Translated in Loewe, *Chinese Ideas of Life and Death*, p. 22.

10 CYLINDRICAL BOX
Lead-glazed earthenware, H. 26.7, Diam. 27.3 cm.
Han dynasty (206 BC-AD 220)
Purchase from the J. H. Wade Fund, CMA 48.214

The molded decoration on the exterior of this box comprises a continuous landscape of steep crags and trees, among which move real and imaginary animals, and immortals. The former include tigers, hares, birds, and dragons. The human-like figures of realized men (zhen ren) or immortals (xian) appear to be communicating directly with the flying dragons and long-tailed birds, and are very similar to the figures stamped on the Han earthenware tomb tile [9]. On a high terrace among the peaks a hare faces a bird; between these two creatures is a vessel. This scene may represent the jade hare of the moon which according to early Daoist beliefs pounded the ingredients of the elixir of immortality. On opposite sides of the box are molded monster (taotie) masks with attached ring handles, in imitation of a bronze original. The fantastic imagery of such vessels reflects a belief in the ethereal soul (hun) that traveled after death to a realm of immortals.

Ceramic boxes of this type—known as lian or zun—were copies of bronze and lacquer vessels used both as food containers and cosmetic boxes. The earthenware clay body of the box is covered with a partially iridescent olive-green lead glaze, colored with copper oxide. The use of a toxic lead glaze indicates that the box was specifically designed for burial in order to accompany the soul into the afterworld.

Molded in several sections, the cylindrical vessel rests on three legs in the shape of bears holding cubs. During the Han dynasty bears were often used in mortuary art, where they functioned as guardian animals. The vessel's flat base is unglazed, revealing the pale, reddish-buff clay body. Comparison with excavated examples suggests that originally the box would have had a lid in the shape of a conical mountain.

PUBLISHED: Jenifer Neils, ed., *The World of Ceramics: Masterpieces from The Cleveland Museum of Art* (Cleveland, 1982), no. 89.

11 MIRROR WITH TLV DESIGNS

Bronze, D. 17.1 cm.
Ca. AD 50-150, Eastern Han dynasty
Worcester R. Warner Collection,
CMA 17.953

Bronze mirrors were often made as guides for the soul in the afterlife. Such mirrors utilized the ancient Chinese symbolism of heaven and earth represented respectively by the circle and square. The reflecting surface of this example is smooth and undecorated, while the back is cast with a dense design of auspicious emblems. The outer circle of the back contains a continuous band of stylized cloud-scrolls. This circle encloses concentric inner circles with zigzag divisions, degree markings, and an inscription referring to immortals (see below). Between these concentric circles and the inner square is a zone with the TLV designs and eight round bosses, among which are the four animals of the cardinal directions in thin, low-relief lines: the dragon of the east, the tiger of the west, the bird of the south, and the dark warrior (a tortoise and snake) of the north. Each of these creatures is paired with another animal, either a deer or a bird.

The name of the TLV classification derives from the geometric shapes that divide up the zone between the outer circles and the inner square. These shapes have been interpreted as representations of cosmological features, including the four cardinal compass points (the Ts) and four corners of the heavens (the Vs).[1] The Ls may function as markers to align the outer circular band of heaven with the Ts marking the cardinal points of the inner earth square. The TLV shapes are believed to have been borrowed from the designs on divining boards of the Han dynasty, known as shi.[2] These were used by diviners to orient an individual's position and cosmological status with regard to heaven and earth. The fixed positioning of the patterns within the inner square and outer circles of the mirror signified the most auspicious orientation of the soul in the afterlife, so that it could find its way to heaven.

In the middle of the mirror is a square containing twelve small bosses interspersed with the characters of the twelve earth branches of the Chinese zodiac.[3] At the very center is a large round boss, perforated horizontally for the insertion of a cord. This symbolizes the *axis mundi* that joins heaven and earth.

The mirror's inscription, cast into the inner circle, refers to the immortals to whose realm the soul of the deceased aspires. Undoubtedly an incantation, it reads:

Through the shangfang has this mirror been made, truly it is very fine,[4]
Above there are immortals [xian ren] who do not know death,
When thirsty they drink from the jade springs, when hungry they eat dates,
They float and wander through the subcelestial realm, rambling within the four seas,
Their longevity resembles that of metal and stone, they are the protectors of the state.[5]

As Suzanne Cahill has shown, this inscription is very similar to passages describing immortals in Daoist texts of the evolving Mao Shan, or Great Clarity (Shangqing) sect of Daoism in the late Han and early Six Dynasties periods.[6] The inscription on the TLV mirrors of the late Han dynasty presage the longer mirror inscriptions of the third and fourth centuries AD, represented here by the mirror depicting the powerful Daoist Queen Mother of the West, the goddess Xiwangmu [12].

Previously unpublished.

NOTES:

1. Michael Loewe, *Ways to Paradise: The Chinese Quest for Immortality* (London: George Allen and Unwin, 1979), p. 74.

2. Ibid., p. 83.

3. On the numerological symbolism in the TLV mirrors of the numbers twelve and five (the latter symbolizing the Five Elements, represented by the four animals of the cardinal directions and the central boss, or *axis mundi)*, see ibid., pp. 60, 80-85.

4. The term *shangfang* refers to the casting of the mirror. *Fang* means "method" or "process," while *shang* refers to a specific tuning of ancient Chinese musical instruments and is used here to refer to the three metals that make up the bronze alloy of the mirror (copper, tin, and lead). The shang tuning corresponds to metal, one of the Five Elements (wu xing); see Suzanne Cahill, "The Word Made Bronze: Inscriptions on Medieval Chinese Bronze Mirrors," *Archives of Asian Art*, 39 (1986), 64.

5. The translation is adapted from Bernhard Karlgren, "Early Chinese Mirror Inscriptions," *Bulletin of the Museum of Far Eastern Antiquities*, 5 (1934), no. 215, and Cahill, "The Word Made Bronze," p. 69, n. 13.

6. Cahill, "The Word Made Bronze," pp. 65, 69, n. 13.

12 MIRROR WITH XIWANGMU, QUEEN MOTHER OF THE WEST
Bronze, Diam. 18.5 cm.
Early Six Dynasties Period, ca. third-fourth century AD
The Severance and Greta Millikin Purchase Fund, CMA 83.213

This extraordinary mirror depicts Xiwangmu, the Queen Mother of the West, and her consort Dongwanggong, the Lord Duke of the East. The depiction of Xiwangmu and other Daoist deities on bronze mirrors proliferated after the fall of the Han dynasty in AD 220. This example has a shiny reflecting surface, while its back is divided into three main zones of decoration. Around a central boss representing the *axis mundi* joining heaven and earth is the innermost zone, containing Xiwangmu and Dongwanggong with other figures and animals. The next zone is a band containing fourteen squares with a long inscription, bounded by two bands with sawtooth decoration. The outermost zone comprises two bands: an inner band with animals, immortals, and a boat or chariot; and the outer band with a diamond and scroll pattern.

Xiwangmu, the deity depicted on the left along the horizontal axis of the innermost zone, is a goddess of ancient lineage. Although references to her may ex-

ist among the oracle bones of the Shang dynasty (sixteenth-eleventh century BC), the first clear mention of her is in the early Daoist text the *Zhuangzi* of the third century BC. There she is listed as a deity who has attained the Dao: "The Queen Mother of the West got it [the Dao] and took her seat on Shaoguang [in later writings she lives on Mount Kunlun in the far west]—nobody knows her beginning, nobody knows her end."[1] References of slightly later date not only describe her as having attained immortality but also ascribe to her the ability of bestowing immortality on humans.[2] The earliest physical description of Xiwangmu is contained in the Han dynasty compilation *Classic of Mountains and Seas (Shanhai Jing)*, which portrays her as part human, part animal:

Another three hundred fifty li to the west is a mountain called Jade Mountain. This is the place where the Queen Mother of the West dwells ... her appearance is like that of a human, with a leopard's tail and tiger's teeth.... In her dishevelled hair she wears a sheng [a U-shaped crown].[3]

By the early Six Dynasties Period (ca. third-fourth century AD) the representation of Xiwangmu had changed considerably. She was then shown as completely anthropomorphic, and the only attribute left from her early description is the

sheng, the headdress or crown with which she is often depicted.[4] Accounts of Xiwangmu in early literature often described her as visited by or visiting earthly rulers, including the legendary emperors Yu and Shun, and the historical King Mu of Zhou (r. 1001-846 BC) and Emperor Wudi of Han (r. 140-87 BC).[5] Poets of the Han dynasty wrote of Xiwangmu's paradise on Mount Kunlun, complete with ornate palaces, trees of jade, and the fabulous Turquoise Pond. The tigers and dragons depicted on the mirror also appear in early literary descriptions as forming the two sides of Xiwangmu's throne.[6] Thus, while she rules over the West, her union with Dongwanggong ensures that her spiritual domain is boundless, for the tiger and dragon respectively symbolize west and east, in addition to Yin and Yang.

The earliest mirror inscription to mention Xiwangmu dates to AD 106.[7] Such inscriptions associate the goddess with longevity, high office, and the bestowal of material rewards. In the Six Dynasties Period Xiwangmu was incorporated in the orthodox Mao Shan sect of Daoism as its highest female deity and the ultimate manifestation of the Yin force.[8]

The figure corresponding to Xiwangmu to the right of the horizontal axis is her consort Dongwanggong. Both deities are attended by feathered immortals and beasts on either side, and their mutual positioning suggests their direct interaction. In Daoist mythology the two deities met once a year on the seventh night of the seventh month (the Double Seventh), as did the Weaving Maiden and the Herd Boy (see [19]). Their yearly meeting represented the coming together of Yin and Yang, the seasonal union needed for the periodic re-creation of the universe.

The figures along the vertical axis are not as easily identified. The figure at the top, however, can be tentatively identified as the famous qin master Bo Ya, from the musical instrument in his lap. Only one person, Zhong Ziqi, was able to understand the depths of Bo Ya's music, and when his friend died, Bo Ya broke his qin. His appearance on the mirror may symbolize the attachment of the relatives who commissioned the mirror to the deceased. The figure at the bottom of the mirror is unidentified but is supported by the head of a tiger or bear, both guardian animals.[9] The deities, ancillary figures, beasts, and four small bosses (perhaps representing the four corners of the heavens) appear against a ground of interlacing designs of bars and circles executed in low relief.[10]

Surrounding the principal zone of decoration is a band with fourteen squares containing an inscription, enclosed by bands of sawtooth designs. The latter may represent the mountain ranges that surround Xiwangmu's paradise on Mount Kunlun. The inscription, which is partially covered by patination, reads:

I have made this bright mirror,
Secluded, I have refined the three shang
[metals].[11]
I have matched and depicted the myriad limits,
I have followed proper precedent and the Dao.
I respectfully present it to the worthy and virtuous,
I have engraved and carved without end.
In all affairs, may the Yang force dominate,
May your happiness and prosperity be extended and bright.
May you have wealth, nobility, peace, and happiness,
May your sons and grandsons be numerous and prosperous ...
May the worthy one be lofty and illustrious.
May the lord become a duke or a minister,
May the master's destiny be long.[12]

The outer band with the immortals, animals, and boat or chariot may depict a journey to Xiwangmu's paradise across the "Weak Waters" surrounding Mount Kunlun.

PUBLISHED: Anneliese Gutkind Bulling, *The Decoration of Mirrors of the Han Period: A Chronology* (Ascona: Artibus Asiae, 1960), pp. 95-96, pl. 79. Sotheby Parke Bernet, *Important Chinese Works of Art: The Collection of Mr. and Mrs. Richard C. Bull* (New York, December 6, 1983), lot 8.

NOTES:
1. Burton Watson, *The Complete Works of Chuang Tzu* (New York: Columbia University Press, 1968), p. 82.

2. For a full discussion of Xiwangmu in early Chinese texts, see Suzanne Cahill, "The Image of the Goddess Hsi Wang Mu in Medieval Chinese Literature" (Ph.D. diss., University of California, Berkeley, 1982), chap. 1.

3. Translated in ibid., p. 11.

4. For a full discussion of the sheng and its associations with weaving, see Michael Loewe, *Ways to Paradise: The Chinese Quest for Immortality* (London: George Allen and Unwin, 1979), pp. 103-105.

5. Cahill, "The Image," pp. 9-10, 34-35.

6. Ibid., p. 23.

7. Ibid., pp. 24-25.

8. Ibid., pp. 25-26.

9. The tiger is mentioned as a guardian animal that devours demons in the Han dynasty text *Lun heng* by the philosopher Wang Chong (AD 27-ca.100); see Derk Bodde, *Festivals on Classical China* (Princeton: Princeton University Press, 1975), p. 128. As for the bear, in late Han funerary reliefs there is sometimes depicted a figure wearing bearskin rugs and a mask. This has been identified by E. Chavannes as the exorcist, or fang-xiangshi, whose function when depicted in funerary art was to purify the tomb and protect the deceased and his possessions from evil spirits; see Bodde, pp. 75-138, and Patricia Berger, "Rites and Festivities in the Art of Eastern Han China: Shantung and Kiangsu Provinces" (Ph.D. diss., University of California, Berkeley, 1980), pp. 30-37.

10. In the account of Xiwangmu in "The Register of the Collected Transcendents of the Fortified Walled City," the paradise of Kunlun is described as having a Mysterious Orchard Garden. This was a mineral garden where the plants were made of precious stones and metals. Among the plants grew "white bracelet trees" that bore stone or jade bracelets. In certain accounts of Xiwangmu's meetings with humans, she gives a jade circlet that bestows immortality. It is possible that the interlacing designs on the mirror represent the courtyard of Xiwangmu with its "bracelet trees" on Mount Kunlun; see Cahill, "The Image," pp. 25, 72-73, 101, n. 40.

11. See [11], n. 4.

12. This inscription is similar to that on a mirror in the Sumitomo Collection, Kyoto, published in Naito Torajiro, et al., *Sen-oku sei-sho* (Kyoto, 1934), pp. 186-187, pl. 39. An identical inscription is translated in Bernhard Karlgren, "Early Chinese Mirror Inscriptions," *Bulletin of the Museum of Far Eastern Antiquities*, 6 (1934), 55-57, no. 177.

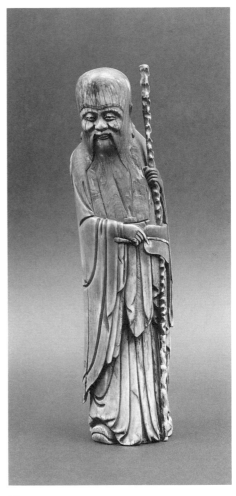

41

13 SHOULAO, THE GOD OF LONGEVITY
Ivory, H: 32.4 cm.
Ca. 1580-ca. 1644, late Ming dynasty
Bequest of James Parmelee, CMA 40.691

The figure of Shoulao (Old Longevity) is dressed in a flowing Daoist robe, leans on a gnarled staff, and holds a fan in one hand. Following convention, he has a large, domed cranium, a fine beard, and three long wrinkles over his eyebrows. His mouth is opened slightly in a smile, revealing an upper row of teeth. His expression is one of benign sagacity.

As with many other Daoist gods, Shoulao was early on associated with a star, and was thus also known as the Star of Longevity, or Shouxing. In addition, he was known as the Old Man of the South Pole, or Nanji laoren, and was believed to reside in the star Canopus. As Mary Fong has shown, the earliest mention of this stellar deity occurs in the early Han dynasty historian Sima Qian's *Shi ji* (early first century BC):

The huge (bright) star located lower than the Wolf Star in the southeast is called the Old Man of the South Pole. When it appears, the nation enjoys peace; when it does not appear, military men rise up. It is seen regularly around the time of the autumnal equinox in the south.[1]

Sima Qian's account suggests that by the Han dynasty the deity was conceived of in anthropomorphic terms.[2] During the reign of the Tang dynasty emperor Xuanzong (r. 713-756), the worship of Shouxing was imperially sanctioned, and a Star of Longevity Altar (Shouxing tan) was erected for this purpose in Chang'an, the Tang capital.[3] In later pictorial art, Shoulao is occasionally shown holding a scroll, in which are recorded the lengths of peoples' lives.[4]

The depiction of Daoist deities in ivory became increasingly popular during the Ming and Qing dynasties. This fine example of Ming ivory carving is cut from a single tusk. The surface has darkened with age and has a rich, golden-brown patina. The figure curves slightly to one side, following the natural curvature of the tusk from which it was carved.

PUBLISHED: William Watson, ed., *Chinese Ivories from Shang to Qing* (London: Oriental Ceramic Society, 1984), no. 96.

NOTES:
1. Mary H. Fong, "The Iconography of the Popular Gods of Happiness, Emolument, and Longevity (Fu Lu Shou)," *Artibus Asiae*, 44, nos. 2-3 (1983), 160.

2. Ibid.

3. Ibid., p. 161.

4. Watson, ed., *Chinese Ivories*, no. 91.

42

14 THE IMMORTAL LI TIEGUAI
Bronze, H. 41.8 cm.
Signed "Su Wennan," ca. early seventeenth century AD, late Ming dynasty
Cornelia Blakemore Warner Fund, CMA 73.158

One of the best-known of the Eight Immortals, Li Tieguai was believed to have lived during the Sui dynasty at the end of the sixth century AD. He is often seen in Chinese painting from the Yuan dynasty onward (see Figure XIIa). The story of his transformation into a crippled beggar follows:

Li Tieguai had an eminent disposition. He attained the Dao at an early age. While cultivating realization in a mountain cave, Li Laojun [Laozi] and Master Wanqiu [an immortal of the Shang dynasty] often descended [from heaven] to his mountain retreat, where they instructed him in Daoist teachings.

One day he was about to attend a meeting with Laojun on Mount Hua [the sacred peak in Shaanxi Province]. Li said to his disciple, "My physical body will remain here—if my ethereal soul [hun] does not return in seven days, you may cremate my body." On the sixth day the disciple's mother fell ill and he had to rush home, so he cremated the body. On the seventh day Li's spirit returned, but his body was gone and he was not pleased. He thereupon possessed the corpse of a man who had starved to death, and rose up. Because of this, his form is that of a crippled man—but he was not like this originally.[1]

This statue of Li Tieguai is made of thickly cast bronze. The immortal is barefoot, dressed in tattered robes, and leans on a crutch, the lower end of which has broken off. Around his waist is a belt of leaves, and a double-gourd hangs to one side. The diadem on his head signifies his immortal status. In his left hand he carries a ball or jewel. His ribs are prominent, and his face has a wild, skeptical expression. A seal-script inscription incised in a square on the figure's back reads: "Made by Su Wennan" (Su Wennan Zhi). This name is unrecorded.

PUBLISHED: *Handbook of The Cleveland Museum of Art* (Cleveland, 1978), p. 355.

NOTE:
1. Wang Shizhen, comp., *Liexian quanzhuan*, chap. 1:2b, reprinted in *Zhongguo gudai banhua congkan* (Shanghai, 1961).

15 THE IMMORTAL HE XIAN'GU
Boxwood, L. 14.4 cm.
Ca. eighteenth century AD, Qing dynasty
Severance and Greta Millikin Purchase
Fund, CMA 76.60

This finely carved boxwood image represents He Xian'gu, one of the Eight Immortals. He Xian'gu was born in the early Tang dynasty (618-906) in Guangzhou, south China.[1] Once during the reign of the usurper Empress Wu Zetian (r. 684-704) she dreamt that an immortal instructed her to eat powdered mica, saying that her body would become light as a feather and live forever. After eating the mica, she vowed she would never marry. She often roamed among mountains and valleys, where she gathered food for her mother. Later on she abstained from grains (a standard Daoist technique of self-purification), and her speech became very strange. Empress Wu sent an emissary to summon her to court, but he lost his way. Finally, during the Jinglong reign period (707-710), He Xian'gu ascended to heaven as an immortal.

In this miniature sculpture, He Xian'gu is shown floating in a log raft. Dressed in a long robe with her hair tied in a chignon, she holds in her hands a ruyi scepter in the shape of a lingzhi mush-

room of immortality (see [24]). In front of her is a basket filled with stalks of bamboo and mushrooms; on the basket rests a hoe. Just behind her is a double-gourd, a common attribute of immortals. Accompanying this sculpture is an ivory base which has been dyed green and carved to represent swirling waves.

PUBLISHED: "Year in Review for 1976," *The Bulletin of The Cleveland Museum of Art*, 64 (February 1977), no. 167, p. 79, rpr. p. 65.

NOTES:
1. *Sancai tuhui* (1607), chap. 11:23a-b.

43

16 BOWL WITH DAOIST PARADISE
Blue-and-white porcelain, Diam. 19.8 cm.
Xuande period (1426-1435), Ming dynasty
John L. Severance Fund, CMA 62.260

The principal decoration on the exterior of this bowl depicts a Daoist paradise with two female immortals flying on phoenixes among billowing clouds, pavilions, and pine-covered mountains. This almost certainly represents the paradise of the Kunlun Mountains, ruled by the Queen Mother of the West (Xiwangmu) and the Jade Maidens (see also [17]). Conceivably the bowl was originally part

of a set presented to a woman of the imperial palace on her birthday, for Xiwangmu was a patron deity of women as well as a goddess of longevity.

The bowl is an excellent example of blue-and-white porcelain of the Xuande reign of the early Ming dynasty, considered by traditional Chinese connoisseurs to be one the finest periods of blue-and-white porcelain production. It is completely covered by a transparent glaze, with the exception of the footring, where the finely levigated porcelain body is visible. The designs are painted in underglaze cobalt oxide around the exterior, while the interior is plain. The high foot-

ring is surrounded by a classic scroll. On the base is a six-character standard script reign mark of the Xuande emperor: "Made in the Xuande reign of the great Ming dynasty" (Da Ming Xuande nian zhi).

PUBLISHED: *An Exhibition of Blue-and-White Decorated Porcelain of the Ming Dynasty* (Philadelphia: Philadelphia Museum of Art, 1949), no. 52.
Exhibition of Chinese Art (Venice: Alfieri, 1954), no. 650.
Jenifer Neils, ed., *The World of Ceramics: Masterpieces from The Cleveland Museum of Art* (Cleveland, 1982), no. 125.

17 VASE WITH XIWANGMU AND THE FESTIVAL OF THE PEACHES OF IMMORTALITY

Porcelain with overglaze *famille verte* enamels, H. 73.9 cm.
Kangxi period (1662-1722), Qing dynasty
Bequest of John L. Severance, CMA 42.654

The main decoration of this enormous vase occupies a panel wrapped around the body and portrays the Festival of the Peaches of Immortality (Pantao hui) in the Kunlun Mountain paradise of Xiwangmu, Queen Mother of the West

[12]. Xiwangmu is shown standing near the bank of the Turquoise Pond (Yao chi), accompanied by four Jade Maidens (Yu nü) and a phoenix, her vehicle. Two of the attendants hold long fans over Xiwangmu's head, both to protect her from the sun and to signify her royal status. Xiwangmu is dressed in an ornate robe decorated with gilt seal-script characters reading: "longevity" (Shou).

A deer pulling a cart containing ripe peaches and vases of flowers approaches the goddess; seven young women accompany the cart. Below, in the immediate foreground, six more women ride in a log raft carrying peaches, while a solitary

maiden follows on a floating flower petal. Beyond the latter figure a stream flows from an underground cavern. The remainder of this scene includes a steep cliff with hoary pine trees and swirling clouds. Nearby are cranes and deer, both symbols of longevity.

The peaches from the trees that blossom once every three thousand years in Xiwangmu's paradise conferred immortality on the person that ate them, and thus function here as a longevity symbol. The peach also symbolizes fertility in China and signifies the expressed desire for abundant progeny. The Han dynasty courtier Dongfang Shuo, who served the fanatical Daoist Emperor Wudi (r. 140-87 BC), was said to have successfully stolen the peaches from Xiwangmu's paradise, thereby becoming an immortal.[1] The theme of the festive gathering of the peaches of immortality was often depicted in painting and ceramics of the Ming and Qing dynasties.[2]

The *famille verte* enamel technique of this vase can be dated to the high Kangxi period (ca. 1690-1720). The enamel palette includes the standard three shades of green (from which the name of the style derives), aubergine, blue, red, yellow, and gold painted over a transparent glaze. The footring is smoothly bevelled and unglazed, enclosing a glazed base with two concentric circles painted in underglaze blue. The neck and shoulder are decorated with stylized floral and geometric motifs, as well as horizontal bands with plum blossoms over cracked ice and panels with flowers of the four seasons. A horizontal band above the footring is also decorated with stylized floral motifs.

Previously unpublished.

NOTES:
1. Suzanne Cahill, "The Image of the Goddess Hsi Wang Mu in Medieval Chinese Literature" (Ph.D. diss., University of California, Berkeley, 1982), pp. 34-35.

2. See, for example, *Eight Dynasties of Chinese Painting*, no. 142.

44

18 DISH WITH ISLE OF THE IMMORTALS
Porcelain with overglaze enamels and underglaze blue decoration, Diam. 21.2 cm. Qing dynasty, mark and period of Yongzheng (1723-1735)
Fanny Tewksbury King Collection, CMA 56.709

At the center of this dish is a roundel depicting a Daoist paradise island with an elaborate palace, surrounded by clouds and rolling waves. This probably represents Penglai, the isle of the immortals in the Eastern Sea. In the foreground three male deities are shown crossing the waves on a cloud. These are the Three Stars: the God of Longevity, Shouxing (Shoulao); the God of Emolument, Luxing; and the God of Good Fortune, Fuxing. On another cloud is a goddess with an attendant holding a scroll. The goddess may represent Xiwangmu, who was worshipped as a controller of human destiny and a deity who revealed important Daoist scriptures to humans.[1] The cranes flying in the air also symbolize longevity.

The exterior of the dish is decorated with a continuous band of rolling waves in blue under a pale green overglaze wash. Among the waves are two large Taihu rocks and diagonally arranged bands of clear glaze. Above the waves appear swirling clouds and bats painted in iron-red enamel, with a pale blue wash above representing the sky.

The symbolism of the dish expresses the wish for good fortune and longevity, and it is possible that this and similar dishes in other collections were designed for an imperial birthday. Of the Three Stars, Shouxing has the oldest history in Chinese culture, first appearing in the Han dynasty.[2] One of the earliest mentions of the Three Stars as a group appears in a drama by the early Ming dynasty prince Zhu Youdun (1379-1439), a son of the first Ming emperor.[3] These three deities are often depicted in Chinese paintings of the Ming and Qing dynasties, as well as on ceramics (Figure 18a). The presence of Xiwangmu (if indeed it is she) near an immortals' isle in the Eastern Sea, while somewhat anomalous, may be a tribute to her widespread popularity as a powerful Daoist goddess of longevity.[4]

The short reign of the Qing dynasty Yongzheng emperor has long been considered one of the high points in the history of later Chinese ceramics. This dish is decorated in the dove-tailed colors palette (doucai), which consists of green, yellow, and red overglaze enamel washes applied over fine-lined underglaze blue designs. It represents the finest porcelain made for the imperial court in the Yong-

45

Figure 18a. *The Three Stars.* Hanging scroll, ink on silk. Attributed to Zheng Dianxian, early sixteenth century, Ming dynasty. Smithsonian Institution, Freer Gallery of Art.

zheng period. With the exception of the thin, bevelled footring, the dish is covered with a shiny transparent glaze. The base has a six-character Yongzheng reign mark within a double circle.

Previously unpublished.

NOTES:

1. Suzanne Cahill, "The Image of the Goddess Hsi Wang Mu in Medieval Chinese Literature" (Ph.D. diss., University of California, Berkeley, 1982), pp. 12, 26.

2. Mary H. Fong, "The Iconography of the Popular Gods of Happiness, Emolument, and Longevity (Fu Lu Shou)," *Artibus Asiae*, 44 (1983), nos. 2-3, pp. 160-161.

3. Ibid., p. 185.

4. See [12], [17].

46

19 RAFT-CUP

Silver, L. 20.5 cm., dated AD 1345
Zhu Bishan (active ca. 1328-1368), Yuan dynasty
John L. Severance Fund, CMA 77.7

This silver wine cup was made by the Yuan dynasty silversmith Zhu Bishan in AD 1345. A native of Jiaxing in Zhejiang Province, Zhu Bishan, also known as Zhu Huayu, was active between 1328 and 1368. Zhu Bishan was famous during his lifetime for his work in silver, and is recorded as having made a wine cup in the shape of a lingzhi mushroom of immortality for the connoisseur Ke Jiusi (1290-1343). He also made a series of wine cups in the shapes of crabs and shrimp.[1]

Zhu's raft-cup was initially cast, and then details were engraved into the surface. The cup is in the shape of a hollow log raft in which a man is seated. This figure, who leans back in the cup, is dressed in a robe with his stomach bared, and looks heavenward with a beatific expression. In his right hand is a rectangular stone, inscribed with three characters in seal script reading: "Loom-supporting stone" (Zhi ji shi). There are four other inscriptions in seal script on the back and bottom of the cup. The longest is this poem:

He wanted to go to the Silver River but was separated by the barriers on high,
While his contemporaries recklessly talked of reaching the Bay of Silver.
Why did he not seek the brocade of the Grandchild of Heaven?
He returned instead with a slab of the loom-supporting stone.

This is followed by an engraved seal: "Bishan." The other three inscriptions are: "Raft cup" (Cha bei), "The year yiyou of the Zhizheng reign [1345]" (Zhizheng yiyou nian), and "Made by Zhu Huayu" (Zhu Huayu zao).

It is clear from the poem that the figure in the raft is an idealized depiction of the Han dynasty explorer Zhang Qian, who between 139 and 126 BC traveled through Central Asia to Bactria.[2] Later legends embroidered on his exploits, claiming that in fact Zhang had ridden a raft to the source of the Yellow River and had found himself floating on the Milky Way, or "River of Heaven." This tale is alluded to in Zhu Bishan's poem, in which the Silver River and Bay of Silver refer to the Milky Way. The Grandchild of Heaven in the third line refers to Zhi Nü, the Weaving Maiden who lived in the star Vega. Once a year, on the seventh of the seventh month, she crossed the Milky Way on a bridge of magpies to meet her lover, Qian niu (the Herd Boy), who lived

in the star Altair.[3] As her name implies, the Weaving Maiden created divine textiles on her loom. Zhu Bishan questions why Zhang Qian, having floated to the Milky Way, brought back only the stone that supported her loom, instead of one of her celestial brocades.

The theme of Zhang Qian riding a log raft on the Milky Way was well-known in Chinese poetry of the Yuan dynasty.[4] The depiction of the figure in the raft is also related to early renditions of Daoist deities riding in similar log rafts.[5] The silver cup thus functions as a symbolic conduit to the heavens, populated by star deities. Immortals traveled freely among the stars, and the figure of Zhang Qian in the raft represents the potential for mortals to communicate with this higher realm.

During the early Qing dynasty, this cup was owned by the great collectors Sun Chengze (1592-1676) and Gao Shiqi (1645-1704). From Gao's collection the cup entered the Qing imperial collection, where it remained until 1860. In that year the cup was taken by British troops from the Summer Palace in Beijing, and in the early twentieth century it entered the collection of Sir Percival David.[6] The only other authentic Zhu Bishan raft-cup that survives today is in the Palace Museum, Beijing.[7]

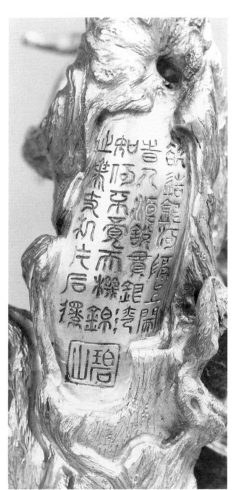

PUBLISHED: Sherman E. Lee and Wai-kam Ho, *Chinese Art under the Mongols: The Yüan Dynasty (1279-1368)* (Cleveland: The Cleveland Museum of Art, 1968), no. 37.

NOTES:
1. For a discussion of Zhu Bishan and his wine cups, see Zheng Minzhong, "Zhu Bishan longcha ji" (A record of Zhu Bishan and his dragon-rafts), *Gugong bowuyuan yuankan*, 1960, no. 2, pp. 165-168.

2. Jeannette Mirsky, ed., *The Great Chinese Travelers* (Chicago and London: University of Chicago Press, 1964), pp. 13-24.

3. Edward H. Schafer, *Pacing the Void: T'ang Approaches to the Stars* (Berkeley: University of Chicago Press, 1977), pp. 143-144.

4. Chen Bangyan, *Lidai tihua shilei* (1708), chap. 35:11b-12a.

5. Lee and Ho, *Chinese Art under the Mongols*, no. 37.

6. R. L. Hobson, "A Silver Cup of the Yüan Dynasty," *Burlington Magazine*, 22 (December 1912), 154.

7. Zhu Jiajin, *Guo bao* (Hong Kong: Shangyu yinshu guan, 1984), pp. 198-199.

20 JADE BOWL WITH PROCESSION OF IMMORTALS
Nephrite, Diam. 15.9 cm.
Jin or Yuan dynasty, thirteenth-fourteenth century AD
Anonymous Gift, CMA 52.510

The main design encircling this jade bowl depicts a procession of three male Daoist immortals with female attendants. It is conceivable that these are early representations of the Three Stars, since the figure with a domed cranium is shown with a scroll (possibly Shouxing with the book listing the lengths of people's lives) and another figure stands next to a deer (a homonym for *lu*, or emolument, the name of another of the Three Stars, Luxing; see [18]). The date of the bowl corresponds roughly to the emergence of the concept of the Three Stars (the Gods of Longevity, Emolument, and Good Fortune) in literature of the fourteenth century. The female attendants are shown holding fans and offerings, including a miniature jade boulder in a basin (*penjing*).

Jade has always been considered to have divine properties in China, and the history of jade carving extends into Neolithic times. Among other things, Daoists believed that jade could retard the deterioration of the corpse after death. In later Chinese history jade was often used in Daoist regalia and for ritual vessels.

Carved from a single block of jade, this bowl has two handles in the shape of female immortals. The interior has a slanting key fret band below the lip and is otherwise plain with several natural flaws in the translucent stone. The exterior has a key fret around the raised footring and borders of cloud collars around the lip and above the foot.

PUBLISHED: Sherman E. Lee and Wai-kam Ho, *Chinese Art under the Mongols: The Yüan Dynasty* (Cleveland, 1968), no. 298.
James C. Y. Watt, *Chinese Jades from Han to Ch'ing* (New York: Asia Society, 1980), no. 131.

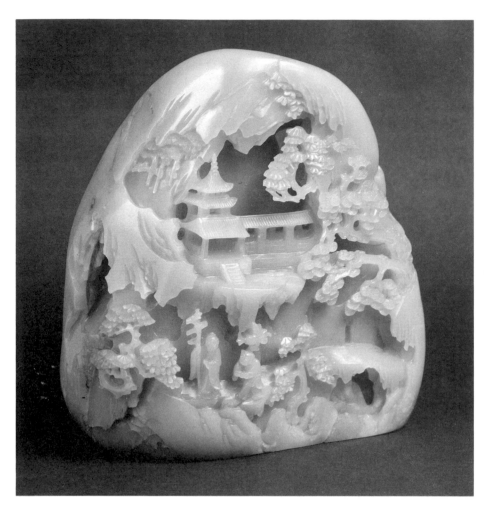

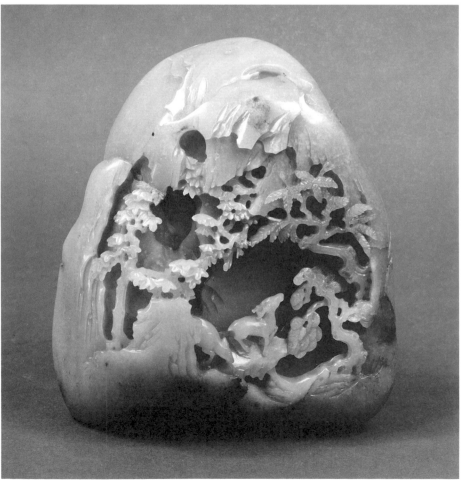

21 JADE MINIATURE MOUNTAIN
Nephrite, H. 17.5 cm.
Qing dynasty, eighteenth century AD
Anonymous Memorial Gift, CMA 41.594

Both sides of this miniature jade mountain depict a Daoist paradise. The translucent nephrite has a rich green color and is deeply carved. On the front a bearded immortal with a staff walks along a path, accompanied by a servant carrying a cluster of peaches (symbols of immortality; see [17]). Above these figures appears a pavilion, built at the front of a grotto among wutong (*Dryandra cordifolia)* and pine trees. The back depicts a pair of deer (symbols of longevity) emerging from another grotto, surrounded by more wutong and pine trees.

Jade miniature mountains are mentioned in literature as early as the twelfth century AD but may have appeared as early as the Tang dynasty.[1] Few large carved boulders, over six inches tall, antedate the seventeenth century AD.[2] Their generic title, "mountains of longevity" (shou shan), reflects the close connection in China between jade and concepts of immortality. The carving of miniature jade mountains reached its height in the Qing dynasty, during the reign of the Qianlong Emperor (r. 1736-1795). This example can be dated to that period on the basis of its high quality and the style of carving.[3]

PUBLISHED: Howard Hollis, "Three Ch'ien-lung Jades," *The Bulletin of The Cleveland Museum of Art*, 29 (October 1942), 127.
William Watson, *L'Art de L'Ancienne Chine* (Paris: Lucien Mazenod, 1979), color pl. 162.

Notes:
1. Berthold Laufer, *Jade: A Study in Chinese Archaeology and Religion* (Chicago: Field Museum of Natural History, 1912; reprint New York: Dover Publications, 1974), p. 331.

2. James C. Y. Watt, *Chinese Jades from Han to Ch'ing* (New York: Asia Society, 1980), p. 27.

3. Compare the Qing dynasty jade miniature mountains published in René-Yvon Lefebvre d'Argencé, *Chinese Jades in the Avery Brundage Collection*, 2d rev. ed. (San Francisco: Asian Art Museum, 1977), pls. 64-67.

22 INK CAKE WITH WANG ZIQIAO
Attributed to Fang Yulu
Probably late Ming or Qing dynasty (ca. seventeenth-eighteenth century AD),
Diam. 5.4 cm.
Gift of Henry W. Kent, CMA 42.233

The brief biography of the immortal Wang Ziqiao in the *Liexian quanzhuan* of 1598 is based on the text of the fourth-century *Biographies of Immortals and Spirits (Shenxian zhuan)*, once attributed to the Daoist alchemist Ge Hong of the Six Dynasties Period:

Wang Ziqiao was the eldest son of Lingwang [King Ling] of the Zhou dynasty [r. 571-545 BC]; his original given name was Jin. He excelled at playing the sheng, with which he made sounds like phoenixes' calls. Once he traveled between the Yi and Luo Rivers [in Henan Province]. The Daoist Fuqiugong took him to the top of Mount Song, where he lived for over thirty years. Later he saw Bo Liang, to whom he said, "You can tell my family that on the seventh day of the seventh month they should wait for me at the top of Mount Gou." On the appointed day he mounted a white crane and flew to the top of the mountain. Although he was visible, no one could reach him. He bowed his head, taking leave of his fellow men, and after several days departed the world. Afterward a shrine was dedicated in his honor at the bottom of Mount Gou.[1]

This small round ink cake has a slightly raised edge, within which the designs are molded in low relief. The front, back, and sides are partially gilded. The design on the front depicts Wang Ziqiao playing the sheng while flying on the back of a crane among stylized clouds. At the center of the back is a raised square with four molded seal-script characters: "Supervised and made by [Fang] Yulu" (Yulu jian zhi). Fang Yulu was one of the most famous makers of ink in Xin'an, Anhui Province, during the late Ming dynasty.[2] Fang collected a series of drawings from Anhui artists, including Ding Yunpeng (1547-ca. 1621), and in 1588 produced the *Fang Family Ink Cake Designs (Fangshi mopu)* with woodblock illustrations of ink cake designs.[3] The quality of this manual was ensured by its being printed by the famous Huang family of Xin'an, whose books were among the finest of all late Ming printed editions.

The design of Wang Ziqiao on the crane does not, however, appear in the *Fangshi mopu*, suggesting either that it was made from a separate design by Fang Yulu or that the Cleveland ink cake dates to a slightly later period and that Fang's well-known name was merely copied onto the back. It is possible that the design was inspired by the depictions of Wang Ziqiao in the *Complete Biographies of Immortals (Liexian quanzhuan)* of 1598 or the *Sancai tuhui* encyclopedia of 1607 (Figure 22a).

PUBLISHED: Howard Hollis, "A Gift of Chinese Inks," *The Bulletin of The Cleveland Museum of Art*, 33 (January 1946), 4.

NOTES:
1. Wang Shizhen, comp., *Liexian quanzhuan* (1598), chap. 1:4a; reprinted in *Zhongguo gudai banhua congkan* (Shanghai, 1961).

2. On Fang Yulu, see Wang Chi-chen, "Notes on Chinese Ink," *Metropolitan Museum Studies*, 3, pt. 1 (1930), 126-129, and Hiromitsu Kobayashi and Samantha Sabin, "The Great Age of Anhui Printing" in James Cahill, ed., *Shadows of Mount Huang: Chinese Painting and Printing of the Anhui School* (Berkeley: University Art Museum, 1981), p. 26.

3. On the *Fangshi mopu*, see Sören Edgren, *Chinese Rare Books in American Collections* (New York: China Institute, 1984), no. 29.

23 OCTAGONAL INK CAKE

Green ink, W. 9.2 cm., dated AD 1622
Attributed to Cheng Junfang (Cheng
Dayue, active ca. 1570-ca. 1624), late
Ming dynasty
Gift of Henry W. Kent, CMA 42.232

This heavy cake of green ink is finely molded with designs on the front and back, and has two short clerical-script inscriptions on the sides. The first inscription reads: "Supervised and made by Cheng Dayue" (Cheng Dayue jian zhi); the second: "The second year of the Tianqi reign" (Tianqi er nian). This date corresponds to AD 1622. The ink cake was made in a four-section mold, judging from the mold marks on the sides. The raised edges around the two primary faces are slightly chipped. An ornate seal-script inscription on the back reads: "Receiving the Mandate of Heaven, the Emperor will prosper forever" (Shou tian zhi ming, Huangdi yong chang). This phrase is based on a similar legend, traditionally believed to decorate the seal of Qin Shihuangdi in the third century BC.[1]

The main design on the front consists of twelve emblems, arranged in a circle around a seal-script inscription: "The Twelve Emblems of Youyu" (Youyu shi er zhang). Youyu was the personal name of Emperor Shun, who according to Chi-

nese mythology ruled during the Age of the Five Emperors in high antiquity, before the founding of the Xia dynasty. The traditional dates of Shun's reign are 2255-2205 BC. According to the Yiji chapter of the *Classic of History*, or *Shu Jing*, these twelve emblems decorated the court robes of Emperor Shun.[2] They comprise the sun, moon, a constellation, a mountain, dragons, a pheasant, ritual vessels, aquatic grasses, fire, grains of rice, an axe, and the geometric fu ornament.[3]

Although the section of the *Shu Jing* in which these symbols are listed was written in the early Bronze Age, its correlation to the legendary Emperor Shun is tenuous at best. The designs were often used, however, in the ornamentation of the court robes of later Chinese emperors. The use of such symbols as the sun and moon—representing the complementary forces of Yin and Yang and depicted on the ink cake with the "red bird" of the sun and the "jade hare" of the moon (the latter pounding the elixir of immortality)— illustrates the borrowing of Daoist symbols current during the late Zhou and Han dynasties. Of the symbols shown on the ink cake, the dragon, another Yang emblem, would become the most prominent in the imperial robes of later dynasties.[4] Other Daoist symbols in this

panoply include the stylized constellation, representing the celestial abode of the higher Daoist deities who sanction imperial power on earth, and the mountain, representing both the element earth and the abode of immortals. In addition, fire and metal, like earth, are among the Five Elements of early Daoist thought and are represented here respectively by the stylized flames and the ritual vessels and axe (both likewise symbols of dynastic legitimacy).

Cheng Junfang, also known as Cheng Dayue, was one of the most famous ink producers of the late Ming dynasty.[5] He worked in Xin'an (Shexian), Anhui Province, and was the teacher of Fang Yulu [22]. Anhui was known as the center of the production of ink, paper, brushes, and inkstones (the four treasures of the scholar's studio). Cheng Junfang created a famous manual of ink cake designs called the *Cheng Family Garden of Ink (Chengshi moyuan)* in 1606, from which the design of this ink cake was taken (Figure 23a). Many of the designs in Cheng's manual were lifted directly out of the *Fangshi mopu* of 1588, the ink cake manual by Cheng's pupil and rival Fang Yulu.[6] Many ink cakes made from the designs in both manuals survive today.[7] Since both the original molds and the woodblock designs survived long after the

lifetimes of Cheng Junfang and Fang Yulu, the precise dating of ink cakes attributed to these masters is difficult, and copies of their designs continued to be made into the twentieth century.

Previously unpublished.

NOTES:

1. See *Zhongwen da cidian* (Taipei: Chinese Culture University, 1973), no. 3324.41.

2. Ibid., no. 2741.91.

3. Ibid., no. 49239.

4. See Schuyler Cammann, *China's Dragon Robes* (New York, 1952), and John Vollmer, *In the Presence of the Dragon Throne* (Toronto: Royal Ontario Museum, 1977).

5. On Cheng Junfang, see Wang Chichen, "Notes on Chinese Ink," *Metropolitan Museum Studies*, 3, pt. 1 (1930), 126-129.

6. Sören Edgren, *Chinese Rare Books in American Collections* (New York: China Institute, 1984), no. 30.

7. For a black ink cake with a design identical to that of the Cleveland ink cake, see Paul Moss, *Documentary Chinese Works of Art in Scholar's Taste* (London: Sydney L. Moss, 1983), pp. 200-201. For other examples of ink cakes attributed to Cheng Junfang, see Wang, "Notes," figs. 7, 8.

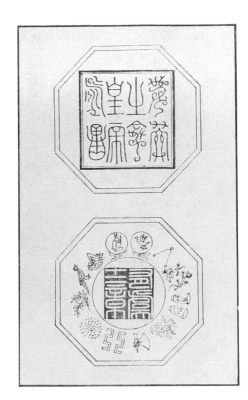

Figure 23a. *Design for an Octagonal Ink Cake* (after *Chengshi moyuan*, 1606).

24 RUYI SCEPTER

Boxwood, L. 38.1 cm.
Eighteenth century AD, Qing dynasty
Cornelia Blakemore Warner Fund,
CMA 70.155

This scepter is realistically carved in the shape of a lingzhi, the mushroom of immortality. The handle is deeply undercut, with small mushroom heads occasionally growing off the main stem. The lingzhi is mentioned in Daoist literature from the Han dynasty onward as a plant that could confer longevity or immortality, and often figured as a key ingredient in elixirs.

The term *ruyi* means "As you wish," a designation associated with wishes for good fortune. As J. Leroy Davidson has shown, the ruyi scepter originated with a type of wand held by an orator or monk, called a "discussion stick" (tanbing).[1] It thus symbolized eloquence in debate and is often seen held by the Buddhist deity Mañjuśrī, the Bodhisattva of Wisdom, from the Six Dynasties Period onward (third-sixth century AD). Several Tang dynasty (eighth century) examples survive in the Shosoin repository in Nara, Japan, which in their plain design suggest that the scepter originally had nothing to do with Daoism. It was only after the Tang dynasty that the ruyi began to be associated in shape with the lingzhi mushroom of immortality and to be a more generalized symbol of good luck. Ruyi scepters of the Ming and Qing dynasties usually take this form and are held by scholars as well as immortals.

PUBLISHED: "Year in Review for 1970," *The Bulletin of The Cleveland Museum of Art*, 58 (February 1971), no. 162, p. 71.

NOTE:
1. J. Leroy Davidson, "The Origin and Early Use of the Ju-i," *Artibus Asiae*, 13, no. 4 (1950), 242. See also E. Zürcher, *The Buddhist Conquest of China*, 2 vols. (Leiden: E. J. Brill, 1959), 2:409, n. 59.

52

25 LINGZHI MUSHROOMS
Album leaf from the *Ten Bamboo Studio Manual of Calligraphy and Painting*
Multi-color woodblock print, 23.7 x 27.9 cm.
Qing dynasty, early eighteenth century
Edward L. Whittemore Fund, CMA 84.45

This multi-color woodblock print depicts several stalks of the lingzhi mushroom (*Polyporus lucidus*) growing next to rocks and grasses on a hillside. The lingzhi is an auspicious symbol of longevity and immortality in China, and often appears in the visual arts from the Song dynasty onward. Lingzhi mushrooms were sacred to the Shangqing and later sects of Daoism, and were believed to have been planted on Mao Shan by the immortal Lord Mao.[1] The lingzhi was also believed to grow on the sacred isles of the immortals in the Eastern Sea. On earth one of the few creatures that could find the lingzhi was the deer, another symbol of longevity.[2]

The volume in which these mushrooms appear illustrates a number of other designs for circular fans. This one is signed "Sketched by Hu Zhengyan" (Hu Zhengyan xie), followed by a seal with the legend "Hu Zhengyan yin." The woodblock illustration is executed in ink with finely modulated washes of yellow, blue, green, ochre, and orange pigments.

A native of Anhui Province, Hu Zhengyan worked primarily in Nanjing in the mid-seventeenth century. His *Ten Bamboo Studio Manual of Calligraphy and Painting (Shizhu zhai shuhua pu)* was the first woodblock-illustrated manual of painting to use the multi-block color printing technique and was first published in 1627 in Nanjing, during the Tianqi reign of the late Ming dynasty.[3] Hu's manual was reprinted several times in the late seventeenth and early eighteenth centuries, and the later editions can sometimes be identified through their use of certain taboo characters in the personal name of the Kangxi emperor (r. 1662-1722) of the early Qing dynasty.[4]

Previously unpublished.

NOTES:
1. Michel Strickmann, "On the Alchemy of T'ao Hung-ching," in Holmes Welch and Anna Seidel, eds., *Facets of Taoism: Essays in Chinese Religion* (New Haven and London: Yale University Press, 1979), pp. 133-134, 146. See also Edward H. Schafer, *Mao Shan in T'ang Times* (Berkeley: Society for the Study of Chinese Religious, 1980), pp. 28-30.

2. C. A. S. Williams, *Outlines of Chinese Symbolism and Art Motives* (Shanghai: Kelly and Walsh, 1941), pp. 328-330.

3. For an excellent introduction to the *Shizhuzhai shuhuapu*, see Jan Tschichold, *Chinese Colour Prints from the Ten Bamboo Studio* (London: Lund Humphries, 1970).

4. Sören Edgren, *Chinese Rare Books in American Collections* (New York: China Institute, 1984), no. 35; see also Robert Treat Paine, "The Ten Bamboo Studio: Its Early Editions, Pictures, and Artists," *Archives of the Chinese Art Society of America*, 5 (1951), 39-54.

Chronological Table of Chinese Dynasties

SHANG	ca. 1600-ca. 1050 BC				
ZHOU	ca. 1050-256 BC				
Western Zhou	ca. 1050-771 BC				
Eastern Zhou	770-265 BC				
Chunqiu (Spring and Autumn Period)	770-476 BC				
Warring States Period	475-221 BC				
QIN	221-207 BC				
HAN	206 BC-AD 220				
Western Han	206 BC-AD 8				
Xin	AD 9-23				
Liu Xuan	23-25				
Eastern Han	25-220				
THREE KINGDOMS	220-280				
Wei	220-265	Shu	221-263	Wu	222-280
JIN	265-420				
Western Jin	265-316				
Eastern Jin	317-420				
SIX DYNASTIES PERIOD	420-589			Southern	
Northern Dynasties	386-581			Dynasties	420-589
				Liu Song	420-479
Northern Wei	386-534			Southern Qi	479-502
Eastern Wei	534-550	Western Wei	535-557	Liang	502-557
Northern Qi	550-557	Northern Zhou	557-589	Chen	557-589
SUI	581-618				
TANG	618-906				
FIVE DYNASTIES PERIOD	907-960				
SONG	960-1279				
Northern Song	960-1126				
Southern Song	1127-1279				
LIAO	916-1125				
JIN	1115-1234				
YUAN	1260-1368				
MING	1368-1644				
QING	1644-1911				

54	An Guo	安國	
	An Lushan	安祿山	
	Anhui	安徽	
	ba xian	八仙	
	Bai Yuchan	白玉蟾	
	baimiao	白描	
	Baiyun guan	白雲觀	
	Baopuzi	抱樸子	
	Beihai	北海	
	Beijing	北京	
	Bian Yongyu	卞永譽	
	Bishan	碧山	
	Bo Liang	栢良	
	Bo Ya	伯牙	
	Cantong ji	參同契	
	Cao Guoqiu	曹國舅	
	cha bei	槎杯	
	Chan	禪	
	Changchun	長春	
	chang sheng	長生	
	Chang'an	長安	

Changsha	長沙
Chen Bangyan	陳邦彥
Chen Hongshou	陳洪綬
Chen Jiru	陳繼儒
Chen Liang Kai	臣梁楷
Chen Ruyan (Weiyun)	陳汝言（惟允）
Chen Wenzhu	陳文燭
Chu	楚
Cui Zizhong	崔子忠
Cui Zizhong yin	崔子忠印
Da Ming Xuande nian zhi	大明宣德年製
daizhao	待詔
dan	丹
Dao	道
Daocang	道藏
Daode Jing	道德經
daoshi	道士
Ding Yunpeng	丁雲鵬
Dong Qichang	董其昌
Dongfang Shuo	東方朔
Donghua	東華

dongtian	洞天	Han	漢
Dongwanggong	東王公	Han Huandi	漢桓帝
Dou	竇	Han Jingdi	漢景帝
Dou Wan	竇綰	Han Wendi	漢文帝
doucai	鬥彩	Han Wudi	漢武帝
Du Mu	都穆	Han Xiangxi	韓湘子
Fang Congyi	方從義	Han Yu	韓愈
Fang Yulu	方玉魯	Han'gu	函谷
Fanghu	方壺	Hangzhou	杭州
fangshi	方士	Hanshan	寒山
Fangshi mopu	方氏墨譜	He Xian'gu	何仙姑
fangxiangshi	方湘氏	Hebei	河北
fengshui	風水	Henan	河南
Fuchun	福春	Heng Shan (Hebei)	恒山
Fuqiugong	浮丘公	Heng Shan (Hunan)	衡山
Fuxing	福星	Hongzhi	弘治
Gao Shiqi	高士奇	hu	笏
Ge Hong	葛洪	Hu Zhengyan	胡正言
Ge Xuan	葛玄	Hu Zhengyan xie	胡正言寫
Geng Zhaozhong	耿昭忠	Hua Shan	華山
Gou Qianzhi	寇謙之	*Huainanzi*	淮南子
Gou Shan	緱山	huan dan	還丹
Gu	顧	Huang	黃
Gu Kaizhi	顧愷之	Huang Di	黃帝
Gu Ying	顧瑛	Huang Gongwang	黃公望
guan	觀	*Huangting Jing*	黃庭經
Guangzhou	廣州	*Huangting neijing jing*	黃庭內景經
Gushe Shan	姑射山	*Huangting waijing jing*	黃庭外景經

hun	魂	Langgan	琅玕
Hunan	湖南	Langye	瑯琊
hundun	混沌	Lao Dan	老聃
Jian Jing	劍經	Laozi	老子
Jiajing	嘉靖	li	里
Jiangsu	江蘇	Li	李
Jiangxi	江西	Li Laojun	李老君
jiao	醮	Li Shan	驪山
jiao mo	焦墨	Li Shaojun	李少君
Jiatai	嘉泰	Li Tieguai	李鐵拐
Jiaxing	嘉興	Li Yangbing	李陽冰
Jin	晋	Li Zhichang	李志常
Jin	金	lian	奩
Jin Shu	晋書	Liang	梁
Jinan	濟南	Liang Kai	梁楷
Jinglong	景龍	Liang Qingbiao	梁清標
Jingming zhongxiao dao	淨明忠孝道	Liang Wudi	梁武帝
Jingyang	旌陽	*Lidai tihua shilei*	歷代題畫詩類
jingli	經歷	*Liexian quanzhuan*	列仙全傳
jinshi	進士	Lin Zhongqing	林仲青
kaishu	楷書	Lin'an	臨安
Kaiyuan	開元	Lingbao	靈寶
Kangxi	康熙	lingzhi	靈芝
Ke Jiusi	柯九思	Liu An	劉安
Kongtong	崆峒	Liu Bang	劉邦
kou fang	口方	Liu Du	劉度
Kunlun	崑崙	Liu Du zhi yin	劉度之印
Lan Caihe	藍采和	Liu Haichan (Xuanying)	劉海蟾（玄英）

56

Liu Jun	劉俊	Ni Zan	倪瓚
Liu Sheng	劉勝	*Nigulu*	妮古錄
Longhu Shan	龍虎山	Niu Shuyu	鈕樹玉
Longquan	龍泉	Pantao hui	蟠桃會
lu (deer)	鹿	Penglai	蓬萊
lu (emolument)	祿	penjing	盆景
Lu	魯	po	魄
Lu Tanwei	陸探微	qi	氣
Lu Xinyuan	陸心源	Qi	齊
Lü Dongbin	呂洞賓	Qian niu	牽牛
Lü Ji	呂紀	Qianlong	乾隆
Lü Wenying	呂文英	qin	琴
Luan	鸞	Qin	秦
Lunheng	論衡	Qin Shihuangdi	秦始皇帝
Luo	洛	Qing	清
Luxing	祿星	*Qinghe shuhua fang*	清河書畫舫
Ma Yuan	馬遠	Qiuyue mohuan	秋月墨幻
Mancheng	滿城	Rijin qingguang	日近清光
Mao Shan	茅山	Ruicheng	芮城
Mawangdui	馬王堆	ruyi	如意
Ming	明	*Sancai tuhui*	三才圖會
Minghualu	明畫錄	Sanjiao	三教
Minghuang	明皇	Shaanxi	陝西
Nanchang	南昌	Shandong	山東
Nanji laoren	南極老人	Shang	商
Nanjing	南京	Shang Xi	商喜
Nanpu	南溥	shangfang	商方
Nei pian	內篇	Shanghai	上海

57

Shangqing	上清	Song Ningzong	宋寧宗
Shanhai Jing	山海經	Song Shan	嵩山
Shanxi	山西	Song Zhenzong	宋真宗
Shaoguang	少廣	Su Wennan	蘇文南
Shen Nong	神農	Su Wennan zhi	蘇文南製
shen ren	神人	Suzhou	蘇州
sheng (instrument)	笙	sui	歲
sheng (crown)	勝	Sui	隋
Shenxian zhuan	神仙傳	Sun Chengze	孫承澤
shi	式	Tai Hu	太湖
Shi Ji	史紀	Tai Shan	泰山
Shide	拾得	Tai Wudi	太武帝
Shigu tang shuhua huikao	式古堂書畫彙考	Tai Yi	太一（乙）
Shihuangdi	始皇帝	Taiping	太平
Shizhu zhai shuhua pu	十竹齋書畫譜	Taiping dao	太平道
shou	壽	*Taiping Jing*	太平經
shou shan	壽山	Taishang laojun	太上老君
Shoulao	壽老	Tan Jing	譚敬
Shouxing	壽星	tanbing	談柄
Shouxing tan	壽星壇	Tang	唐
Shun	舜	Tang Gaozong	唐高宗
Shuxian	叔憲	Tang Gaozu	唐高祖
Sichuan	四川	Tang Muzong	唐穆宗
Sima Chengzhen	司馬承禎	Tang Wuzong	唐武宗
Sima Qian	司馬遷	Tang Xianzong	唐憲宗
Siming	司命	Tang Xuanzong (8th century)	唐玄宗
Song	宋	Tang Xuanzong (9th century)	唐宣宗
Song Huizong	宋徽宗	Tang Zuomei	唐作梅

58

Tao Hongjing	陶弘景	wu xing	五行
Tao Qian (Yuanming)	陶潛（淵明）	wu yue	五岳
Taohuayuan ji	桃花源紀	Wu Zetian	武則天
taotie	饕餮	Wude	武德
Tian shi	天師	wutong	梧桐
Tian shi dao	天師道	*Wuzhen bian*	悟眞編
Tianqi	天啓	Xia Wenyan	夏文彥
Tuhui baojian	圖繪寶鑑	xian	仙
Wang Chong	王充	Xian shan tu	仙山圖
Wang Jiqian	王季遷	Xiang Yuan	項源
Wang Liyong	王利用	Xiang Yuanbian	項元汴
Wang Meng	王蒙	*Xiao Jing*	孝經
Wang Shizhen	王世貞	Xie Youyu	謝幼輿
Wang Xianzhi	王獻之	Xin'an	新安
Wang Xizhi	王羲之	xinhai	辛亥
Wang Zhe	王喆	xingshu	行書
Wang Zhideng	王穉登	xiucai	秀才
Wang Ziqiao	王子喬	Xiwangmu	西王母
Wanqiu	宛丘	Xu Hao	虛耗
Wei	魏	Xu Hui	許翽
Wei Boyang	魏伯陽	Xu Mi	許謐
Wei Huacun	魏華存	Xu Qin	徐沁
Wen Zhengming	文徵明	Xu Xun (Jingyang)	徐遜（旌陽）
Wu Daozi	吳道子	Xuande	宣德
wu dou mi dao	五斗米道	Yan Hui	顏輝
Wu Kuan	吳寬	Yan Liben	閻立本
Wu Meng	吳猛	Yan Shan	燕山
wu wei	無爲	Yang	陽

Selected Bibliography

Chan, Albert. *The Glory and Fall of the Ming Dynasty.* Norman: University of Oklahoma Press, 1982.

Chang, Kwang-chih. *The Archaeology of Ancient China.* 3d ed. New Haven and London: Yale University Press, 1979.

Chang Po-tuan. *The Inner Teachings of Taoism.* Translated by Thomas Cleary. Boston and London: Shambala, 1986.

Ch'en, Kenneth. *Buddhism in China: A Historical Survey.* Princeton: Princeton University Press, 1964.

Cooper, T. C. *Chinese Alchemy.* Wellingborough: The Aquarian Press, 1984.

Eberhard, Wolfram. *A History of China.* 4th ed. Berkeley and Los Angeles: University of California Press, 1977.

Eight Dynasties of Chinese Painting: The Collections of the Nelson Gallery-Atkins Museum, Kansas City, and The Cleveland Museum of Art. Cleveland, 1980.

Fu Shen, et al. *Traces of the Brush: Studies in Chinese Calligraphy.* New Haven: Yale University Press, 1977.

Fung Yu-lan. *A Short History of Chinese Philosophy.* New York: MacMillan, 1948.

Gendai dōshaku jinbutsuga. Tokyo: Tokyo National Museum, 1975.

Gugong shuhua lu. 3 vols. Taipei: National Palace Museum, 1958.

Hay, John. "Huang Kung-wang's 'Dwelling in the Fu-ch'un Mountains': Dimensions of a Landscape." Ph.D. diss., Princeton University, 1978.

_____. *Kernels of Energy, Bones of Earth: The Rock in Chinese Culture.* New York: China Institute, 1985.

Ho, Peng Yoke. *Li, Qi and Shu.* Hong Kong: Hong Kong University Press, 1985.

Jan Yun-hua. "The Silk Manuscripts on Taoism." *T'oung Pao,* 63, no. 1 (1977, 65-84.

Kaltenmark, Max. "The Ideology of the *T'ai-p'ing Ching.*" In *Facets of Taoism,* edited by Welch and Seidel, pp. 19-52.

Kao, Karl S. Y., ed. *Classical Chinese Tales of the Supernatural and the Fantastic.* Bloomington: Indiana University Press, 1985.

Ledderose, Lothar. *Mi Fu and the Classical Tradition of Chinese Calligraphy.* Princeton: Princeton University Press, 1979.

Lee, Sherman E., and Wai-kam Ho. *Chinese Art under the Mongols: The Yüan Dynasty, 1279-1368.* Cleveland, 1968.

Legeza, Laszlo. *Tao: The Chinese Philosophy of Time and Change.* London: Thames and Hudson, 1973.

_____. *Tao Magic: The Chinese Art of the Occult.* London: Thames and Hudson, 1975.

Liu, Da. *The Tao and Chinese Culture.* New York: Schocken Books, 1979.

Loewe, Michael. *Chinese Ideas of Life and Death.* London: George Allen and Unwin, 1982.

Mather, Richard B. "K'ou Ch'ien-chih and the Taoist Theocracy at the Northern Wei Court, 425-451." In *Facets of Taoism,* edited by Welch and Seidel, pp. 103-122.

Miyakawa Hisayuki. "Local Cults around Mount Lu at the Time of Sun En's Rebellion." In *Facets of Taoism,* edited by Welch and Seidel, pp. 83-101.

Morrison, Hedda. *Hua Shan, The Taoist Sacred Mountain in West China: Its Scenery, Monasteries and Monks.* Hong Kong: Vetch and Lee, 1973.

Neill, Mary Gardner. "Mountains of the Immortals: The Life and Painting of Fang Ts'ung-i." Ph.D. diss., Yale University, 1981.

New Archaeoalogical Finds in China. Beijing: Foreign Languages Press, 1978.

Ofuchi Ninji. "The Formation of the Taoist Cannon." In *Facets of Taoism*, edited by Welch and Seidel, pp. 253-267.

Pontynen, Arthur. "The Deification of Laozi in Chinese History and Art." *Oriental Art*, 26, no. 2 (Summer 1980): 192-200.

_____. "The Dual Nature of Laozi in Chinese History and Art." *Oriental Art*, 26, no. 3 (Autumn 1980): 308-313.

Saso, Michael. *The Teachings of Taoist Master Chuang*. New Haven and London: Yale University Press, 1978.

Schafer, Edward H. *Mao Shan in T'ang Times* (Berkeley: Society for the Study of Chinese Religion, 1980).

Sirén, Osvald. *Chinese Painting: Leading Masters and Principles*. 7 vols. London: Lund Humphries, 1956-58.

Sivin, Nathan. *Chinese Alchemy: Preliminary Studies*. Cambridge, Mass.: Harvard University Press, 1968.

Stein, Rolf. "Religious Taoism and Popular Religion from the Second to Seventh Centuries." In *Facets of Taoism*, edited by Welch and Seidel, pp. 53-81.

Steinhardt, Nancy Shatzman, et al. *Chinese Traditional Architecture*. New York: China Institute, 1984. pp. 133-137.

Strickmann, Michel. "The Longest Taoist Scripture." *History of Religions*, 17, nos. 3-4 (February-March 1978): 331-354.

_____. "The Mao Shan Revelations: Taoism and the Aristocracy." *T'oung Pao*, 63, no. 1 (1977): 1-64.

_____. "On the Alchemy of T'ao Hung-ching." In *Facets of Taoism*, edited by Welch and Seidel.

Suzuki Kei. *Chūkogu kaiga sōgo zuroku*. 5 vols. Tokyo: Heibonsha, 1982.

Szuma Chien [Sima Qian]. *Selections from Records of the Historian*. Translated by Yang Hsien-yi and Gladys Yang. Beijing: Foreign Languages Press, 1979.

Waley, Arthur. *The Travels of an Alchemist*. London: n.p., 1931.

_____. *The Way and Its Power: A Study of the Tao Te Ching and Its Place in Chinese Thought*. New York: Grove Press, 1958.

Wang Shizhen, comp. *Liexian quanzhuan*. 1598. Reprint *Zhongguo gudai banhua congkan*. Shanghai: Wenwu chubanshe, 1961.

Ware, James. *Alchemy and Religion in the China of AD 320: The Nei P'ien of Ko Hung*. Cambridge, Mass.: Massachusetts Institute of Technology Press, 1966.

Watson, Burton, trans. *The Complete Works of Chuang Tzu*. New York: Columbia University Press, 1968.

_____. *Early Chinese Literature*. New York: Columbia University Press, 1962.

Watson, William. *The Chinese Exhibition*. London: Times Newspapers, 1974.

Watt, James C. Y. *Chinese Jades from Han to Ch'ing*. New York: Asia Society, 1980.

Welch, Holmes. *Taoism: The Parting of the Way*. Boston: Beacon Press, 1957.

Welch, Holmes, and Anna Seidel, eds., *Facets of Taoism: Essays in Chinese Religion*. New Haven and London: Yale University Press, 1979.

Yoshioka, Yoshitoyo. "Taoist Monastic Life." In *Facets of Taoism*, edited by Welch and Seidel, pp. 229-252.

Yu Jianhua. *Zhongguo hualun leibian*. 2 vols. 1956. Reprint Hong Kong: Zhonghua shuju, 1973.

Index

Numbers in square brackets represent catalogue numbers thus, [8] refers to the hanging scroll *The Peach Blossom Spring* by Liu Du.

Alchemy, 1, 3, 5-7, 10, 14, 29, 54
An Lushan rebellion, 8, 29
Axis mundi, 39, 40

Bai Yuchan, 10, 54
Baiyun guan (White Cloud Monastery), 9, 54
Baopuzi, 6, 54
Bo Ya, 40, 54
Book of Pure Commands of Great Peace, 4
Bowl with Daoist Paradise, [16], 43
Buddha, 9, Figs. VII, VIII
Buddhism, 8, 11, 12, 26
    Chan (Zen), 9, 12, 28
    Vajrayana or Tantric, 10
Buddhist-Daoist debates, 8, 9

Cantong ji (The Threefold Unity), 6, 54
Cao Guoqiu, 11, 54, Fig. XIf
Cao Guoqiu, 11, Fig. XIf
Celestial Master sect, first. See Mao Shan.
Celestial Master or Orthodox Unity sect. See Zhengyi.
Celestial Master Zhang Daoling, [2], 27-28
Cha bei, 54. See also Raft-cup.
Changchun, 11, 54
Chang sheng (techniques of longevity), 3, 33, 54
Chen Hongshou, [1], 18, 26-27, 36, 54
Chen Ruyan (Weiyun), [5], 31-32, 54
Chen Wenzhu, 34, 54
Cheng Junfang (Dayue), [23], 50-51
Chengshi moyuan (Cheng Family Garden of Ink), [23], 50-51; illustration from, 51, Fig. 23a,
Cinnabar (dan), 3, 4, 5-6, 8, 31, 33, 54
Classic of Filial Piety. See *Xiao Jing*.
Classic of Great Peace. See *Taiping Jing*.
Classic of Mountains and Seas. See *Shanhai Jin*.
Classic of the Yellow Court. See *Huangting Jing*.
The Complete Biographies of Immortals. See *Liexian quanzhuan*.

Complete Realization sect. See Quanzhen.
Concealed Instructions for Ascent to Perfection, 7
Confucianism, 6, 12,
Confucius, 2, 9, Fig. VII
Cui Zizhong, [4], 30-31, 54
Cylindrical Box, [10], 38

Dao, 4, 6, 40, 41, 54; defined, 1; union with, 3, 29
Daocang (Daoist canon), 8, 12, 27, 54
Daode Jing (The Way and Its Power), 1, 2, 3, 4, 5, 6-7, 8, 9, 26, 27, 30, 54
Daoism, 1-14 *passim*, 37; imperial patronage of, 8, 9, 11, 14, 28; sects, 5
Daoshi (Daoist priests), 10, 11-12, 54
Dark warrior (a tortoise and snake) of the north, 39
Declarations of the Perfected, 7
Design for an Octagonal Ink Cake, 51, Fig. 23a,
Ding Yunpeng, 49, 54
Dish with Isle of the Immortals, [18], 45-46, color repr. 22
Dong Qichang, 30, 54
Dongfang Shuo, 44, 54
Dongwanggong (Lord Duke of the East), 40, 55
Dou, Empress, 3, 55
Dou Wan, 4, 55
Dragon, 6, 40, 50, Figs. IV, V, of the east, 39, symbol of Dao, 6
Dragon Emerging from the Waves, 5, 6, 7, Fig. V
Duke Wei of Qi. See Wei, Duke of Qi.
Dwelling in the Fuchun Mountains by Huang Gongwang (mention of), 12

Eight Immortals, 10-11, 32, Figs. IX, XIa-h
Elixirs of immortality, 3, 4, 5-6, 7, 27, 31, 33, 50, 51
Essay on Awakening to Reality. See *Wuzhen bian*.

Fang Yulu, [22], 49, 50-51, 55
Fanghu, 37, 55
Fangshi (magicians), 3, 55
Fangshi mopu (Fang Family Ink Cake Designs), 49, 50, 55

63

64

66